Praise for
Fight Fair!

Conflict is common to all marriages. What MOST marriages don't have is a blueprint for resolving conflict when it occurs. Tim and Joy not only share with you THE most effective blueprint, but they will give you the practical tools and coaching needed in marriages today. Buy and apply this book! It'll revolutionize your relationship.

Dr. Dennis Rainey
President, FamilyLife

All couples fight. Tim and Joy Downs offer inspirational and doable coaching for couples who want to strengthen their love in the midst of inevitable conflict.

Dr. Tim Kimmel
Author of *Grace Based Parenting*

TIM & JOY DOWNS

FIGHT FAIR!

WINNING AT CONFLICT WITHOUT LOSING AT LOVE

MOODY PUBLISHERS

CHICAGO

All Scripture quotations, unless otherwise indicated, are taken from the *New American Standard Bible®*, Copyright © The Lockman Foundation 1960, 1962, 1963, 1968, 1971, 1972, 1973, 1975, 1977, 1995. Used by permission.

Scripture quotations marked NIV are taken from the *Holy Bible, New International Version®*. NIV®. Copyright © 1973, 1978, 1984 by International Bible Society. Used by permission of Zondervan Publishing House. All rights reserved.

Scripture quotations marked THE MESSAGE are from *The Message,* copyright © by Eugene H. Peterson 1993, 1994, 1995. Used by permission of NavPress Publishing Group.

Scripture quotations marked NLT are taken from the *Holy Bible, New Living Translation,* copyright © 1996. Used by permission of Tyndale House Publishers, Inc., Wheaton, Illinois 60189, U.S.A. All rights reserved. Published in association with the literary agency of Alive Communications, Inc., 7680 Goddard Street, Suite 200, Colorado Springs, Colorado 80920.

Edited by Cheryl Dunlop (2003) and Pam Pugh (2010)
Interior and cover design: Smartt Guys design

LIBRARY OF CONGRESS CATALOGING-IN-PUBLICATION DATA
Downs, Tim.
    Fight fair! : winning at conflict without losing at love / Tim and Joy Downs.
        p. cm.
    Includes bibliographical references.
    ISBN: 978-0-8024-1428-1
    1. Marriage–Religious aspects—Christianity 2. Conflict management—Religious aspects—Christianity. I. Downs, Joy. II. Title.

BV835.D685 2003
306.872—dc21

                                    2003007613

We hope you enjoy this book from Moody Publishers. Our goal is to provide high-quality, thought-provoking books and products that connect truth to your real needs and challenges. For more information on other books and products written and produced from a biblical perspective, go to www.moodypublishers.com or write to:

Moody Publishers
820 N. LaSalle Boulevard
Chicago, IL 60610

5 7 9 10 8 6

Printed in the United States of America

For Tommy, Erin, and Kelsey

When you marry one day,
may you be humble in victory,
gracious in defeat,
generous to a fault,
and thankful for all
that God has given you.
Remember, "The greatest of all arts
is the art of living together."

We love you.

CONTENTS

A Game Without RULES

DOWNS

"I'm ready to say a definite 'maybe,' but I might want to revisit that later."

A GAME WITHOUT RULES

Try to imagine a game without rules.

Imagine a game of poker where one player holds five cards, but another holds eighteen. Imagine a game of Monopoly where you can rob the bank, break out of jail, and burn your opponent's hotels. Imagine a baseball game where the batter keeps the bat with him as he rounds the bases, just to break up that annoying double play at second base. Or how about a game of Scrabble where you can make up any word you like?

Most games work better with a few guiding principles in place. You would have to search far and wide to find a sport, a game, or even a simple contest with no rules whatsoever.

But there is one.

"What's this?" a husband demands, tossing a receipt onto the kitchen table.

"What's what?" his wife says without looking up.

"Two hundred and fifty dollars! For what?"

"For something I needed," she says indifferently.

"Why would you spend that kind of money without asking me first?"

"How was golf today?" she asks. "What did that set us back—forty, fifty dollars? You never seem to mention the cost of your hobbies, now, do you?"

"I'm talking about *unnecessary* expenses!" he says as his voice begins to rise.

"Why is it that only my expenses are unnecessary?" she shouts back.

"You're wasting our money!" he yells, charging from the room.

"What do you know about money?" she calls after him.

Conflict, which someone has said is the art of disagreeing while still holding hands, is a game without rules. It may sound strange to speak of conflict as a "game," but in a sense it is. Every marital disagreement has two players, a starting point, and a finish line. There is a playing field and a time limit, and there are penalties, fouls, and grounds for disqualification along the way. There are winners and losers too—though in this game, unlike most, both players can win or both can lose.

Right now you may be thinking, *If conflict is a game, then I'd rather not play*. Sorry. Conflict is a part of the true game of Life, and refusing to play is simply not an option. Differences in personality and temperament, multiple time demands, limited resources, and the sheer insanity of modern life all conspire to create occasional (or more than occasional) disagreements between partners. In marriage, conflict simply can't be avoided; the goal, then, is to learn to play the game as pleasantly and productively as possible.

We know a wise grandmother who cautions her grandkids, "Fight nicely." What a concept! For many of us, the very idea of *fighting nicely* is a contradiction in terms. You can fight, or you can be nice; take your pick. But doing both at once is something many couples have never experienced. Believe it or not, it is possible to "fight nicely." That's where clear rules and a good referee come in—and that's what conflict often lacks.

Like the early sport of boxing, conflict between lovers often has a single guiding principle: *Beat the other guy*. In the early days of boxing, the question of *how* to beat the other guy was left entirely to the individual combatants, and liberal interpretations of that rule left many men bloody, broken, or blind. Some, like the gladiators of old, even gave their lives in the arena.

That's why, in the late 1800s, the Marquis de Queensberry thought it was high time someone sat down and penned some rules for the sport of boxing. No more kicking and gouging, he said, and no more hitting below the belt. No head butting is allowed, no rabbit punching, and under no circumstances are you ever allowed to bite off your opponent's ear.

But just because a rule exists, that doesn't mean anyone has to obey it. That's why the Marquis de Queensberry's regulations provided for a referee, a man whose job it was to make sure the rules were followed. To this day, whenever a boxing match is about to begin, a man in a striped shirt steps between the opponents and reviews the basic rules. To break the rules, he reminds them, is to forfeit the contest. The referee's goal is not to prevent the boxers from fighting; on the contrary, he is there to allow them to fight. The referee's goal is not to prevent the conflict from happening, but to make sure the boxers *fight fair*. By doing so, he greatly increases the chances that the boxers will live to fight another day.

But in marital conflict, there are no rules. Maybe that's why there's so much gouging, biting, and hitting below the belt—and maybe that's why so many love relationships perish in the act of disagreeing.

Wouldn't it be great if, when the sparks begin to fly between a husband and wife, a bell would ring, a closet door would fly open, and a man in a striped shirt would step out? Our own personal marital referee!

"You're wasting our money!" the husband yells, charging from the room.

"Foul!" the referee calls out. "Get back in the ring or you're disqualified!"

"What do you know about money?" his wife calls after him.

"That's hitting below the belt!" the referee warns. "One more time and you're out of the game!"

Since we have no referees to supervise our personal conflicts, we have to serve as our *own* referees. But what are the rules we should enforce? What are the errors and pitfalls we should watch for, and what are the behaviors we should encourage? This book is intended to be your own personal *Marquis de Queensberry's Rules for Conflict* in relationships: not a list of rules that *we* think you should apply, but a chance for you and your spouse to agree together on your *own* guidelines for successful conflict. All along the way we'll give you tips, insights, and suggestions that have worked for others, but it's your job to decide what you think will work best for you. At the end of the book is a section entitled "Our Rules." As you finish each chapter, turn back to the "Our Rules" section and record any ideas you agree to apply in your own relationship.

You'll find an entire chapter devoted to "Penalties and Fouls" (chapter 14), behaviors that are unproductive, discouraging, or even downright dangerous to the health of your relationship. We'll give you a chance to identify your *own* fouls—specific words, behaviors, and attitudes that you know from experience to be hurtful or unproductive. In the "Our Rules" section, you'll find a place for you to record your "Personal Fouls," so that you can agree together to avoid them in the future.

By the end of this book, you will have your own personal set of rules for conflict. We encourage you to copy off those pages. Keep your list of guidelines handy to remind you of the things you've agreed together to do—and *not* do—in your next disagreement.

A word of caution: Rules allow a game to be played fairly and efficiently, but no game consists of rules alone. As we'll emphasize over and over in this book, *success in conflict requires more than a set of rules.* It depends even more on the attitudes you bring to the game: humility, generosity, gentleness, and a genuine desire to work things out. If you are intent on being stubborn or on punishing your mate, no set of rules will prevent you from doing so. The rules in this book can improve your *technique* in conflict, but as chapter 5 will remind you, the attitude *behind* the technique is crucial.

Everyone disagrees; that's inevitable. The question is, How can we disagree with those we love but increase the odds that we will live and love to fight another day? How can we learn to "fight fair"?

"How about this: You do 50% of the housework,
I do 10% and we ignore the rest."

WHERE CONFLICTS COME FROM

It's been a long day, a good day, and they've just settled down for a long winter's nap. They smooth and straighten the covers, trade a good-night peck, and reach for their respective light switches. Life is good, the world is at peace, and all is right with the universe—when suddenly she says, ***"Let's not forget to clean the garage next weekend."***

"OK," he says, already halfway to the land of Nod. "Glad to help."

A pause . . .

"What does that mean?"

He tenses. Some primal instinct warns him away, but testosterone causes him to plow ahead like a Labrador into a duck pond.

"What does *what* mean?" he asks.

"'Glad to help.' What do you mean by help?"

His mind races. What could possibly be wrong with the word *help*? Glad to *assist*? Glad to *lend a hand*? Where did he put that thesaurus?

"I just mean that I'm glad to . . . you know . . . clean the garage too."

"You mean you're glad to help me clean the garage. Like cleaning the garage is my job, and you're just helping out."

"Oh, come on, honey; you're just being picky." Another primal instinct ties a knot in his stomach, the same instinct that used to warn his ancestors not to poke the lion with a stick.

"Picky? Did you say picky?"

In the darkness, he hears her sit upright in bed. He feels the warm, protective covers slide away, and somehow the room feels much colder than it was just moments before. . . .

Where do conflicts come from? Probably not from where you think. Most couples tend to put the blame for conflicts on *topics* of disagreement. They assume an argument begins because they cannot agree on:

- **FINANCES**
- PARENTING DECISIONS
- **IN-LAW RELATIONSHIPS**
- SEX
- **POWER AND AUTHORITY**
- WORK DEMANDS
- **SCHEDULING AND PRIORITIES**
- USE OF LEISURE TIME
- **PERSONAL HABITS**
- HOUSEHOLD RESPONSIBILITIES

But have you ever noticed that there's a world of difference between a *difference of opinion* and a *disagreement*? You say "potayto," I say "potahto"; that's just a difference of opinion. You experience no rising anger, no mounting tension, no growing hostility or resentment. "Of course not," you say. "That's because it isn't important." But are all your disagreements about matters of national security? Or have you discovered, as most married couples do, that heated disagreements can erupt over the most mundane and unexpected topics?

THE GATHERING STORM

What is it that turns a minor difference of opinion into a full-fledged disagreement? It has little to do with the topic; a topic serves only as a trigger that gets a conflict under way. Topics attract conflict the way tall buildings attract lightning. It's just a place for the conflict to *ground*; but for lightning to strike at all, there have to be storm clouds gathering above.

To the hapless man in our opening scenario, their midnight misunderstanding was a bolt out of the blue: What got into *her*? But to his wife, this conflict had been building up for months. His offer to "help" with the garage reflected his long-held attitude that all jobs around the house were *her* jobs. When she did them herself, she was simply doing her job; when *he* did them, he was "helping," and he felt that he deserved special recognition. He never *said* as much; it was just his attitude. Over time, there were more and more jobs to do around the house—more of *her* jobs—and her annoyance at his attitude had been building up inside her like an electrical charge. All it needed was one more comment to get the thunderstorm under way.

Sometimes life is so busy and demanding that couples feel like little more than business partners, both faithfully serving the company but rarely meeting after hours. There *are* no "after hours"; in marriage and parenting, the job never really ends. There's always something else to do, and it takes both of you just to cover the bases.

After years of this kind of endless service, couples can begin to feel like train tracks running parallel to each other but never seeming to cross. You're both important, and you both carry your own burdens—but it's lonely to travel endlessly in the same direction just a few feet away from the one you love.

Much is written today about uninvolved parents, passive husbands, and irresponsible wives. But there's another problem that challenges marriages today, a problem that's rarely discussed. It's the problem of involved parents, active husbands, and responsible wives. But how can that be a problem? Aren't those qualities good for children, good for society, good for the world? Yes—but they're hard on a marriage. There are millions of couples today who *aren't* lazy or selfish or uncommitted; they are selfless and tireless and self-sacrificing. They put the kids first, the job first, the church first—they put *everything* first ahead of their own marriage. But when we invest in everything and everyone but *us,* marriage eventually becomes a cold, lonely, and disappointing business—and that's when the storm clouds of conflict begin to darken the skies above.

When you and your mate take time to be together, when you make a practice of encouraging and supporting each other, there is a confidence in the relationship that forms a buffer against misunderstanding and miscommunication—a buffer made of attitudes like:

- **I'm confident of your love for me, even if you haven't told me lately.**

• I know you're trying, even when it doesn't show.
• **I know you mean well, even when it comes out wrong.**
• I think the best of you, even when you fail.
• **I trust you, even when I'm not there with you.**

When you firmly believe—when you really *feel*—that your mate loves, values, and respects you, it's easier to overlook the minor oversights and annoyances that dot the landscape of married life.

But when life gets too busy to allow time together, or when your mate makes no effort to fill your cup, then a vapor of coldness and discouragement begins to condense. Unfortunately, misunderstandings and miscommunications don't diminish just because your schedule is full. On the contrary, they increase; misunderstandings are an inevitable by-product of the breakneck pace of life. *Why did he do that? What did she mean by that? How could he forget* again?

> **INSIGHT**
> **Any idiot can face a crisis; it's this day-to-day living that wears you out!**
> —*Greeting Card*

When there isn't time or energy to discuss your hurts and misunderstandings, a sense of hopelessness begins to grow. Why bring up yet another problem or concern? There wasn't time to deal with the last one. It's easier to simply withdraw, and that's what many of us do, deepening our sense of isolation from one another.

It takes time, energy, and patience to learn what makes your mate feel loved and encouraged.

But when everything comes before *us,* there simply is no time. For many of us, our marriages have become functional, efficient business ventures—but they have little passion or depth behind them. Then that protective buffer against conflict evaporates and a dark cloud of negative attitudes takes its place:

> ***TIP***
> IF YOUR MARRIAGE HAS BEEN JUST A BUSINESS PARTNERSHIP, THEN CREATING AN ATMOSPHERE OF TRUST, RESPECT, AND CONFIDENCE WILL TAKE TIME.

> **INSIGHT**
> Interpersonal climate is the overall feeling, or emotional mood, between people.... Two couples might live in the same apartment complex, have similar jobs, and distribute responsibilities for cleaning, cooking, and shopping in the same way. Yet in one of the relationships, there is constant tension, marked by short and sometimes cutting remarks and frequent flares of temper. In the other relationship the pervasive feeling is comfortable and friendly.... Because interpersonal climate concerns the overall feeling between people, it is the foundation of personal relationships.
> —*From* Interpersonal Communication *by Julia Wood, 245*

1
INSIGHT
Even if we had a
recording of each
conflict, we would
still disagree on
what the words
really meant.

2
INSIGHT
Sometimes it takes a
few moments to sort
out our feelings and
the reasons for them.
It's best to have
that thought through
before opening
our mouths.

3
INSIGHT
The words "I am . . ."
are potent words;
be careful what you
hitch them to. The
thing you're claiming
has a way of
reaching back
and claiming you.
—*A. L. Kitselman*

INSIGHT — Most conflicts are conflicts waiting to happen.

- **I'm unsure of your love for me, because you don't express it.**
- I'm not sure you're really trying, because it doesn't show.
- **I think you do it on purpose, because it keeps coming out wrong.**
- I think less of you when you fail.
- **I don't trust you unless I'm there with you.**

Conflicts come from the atmosphere of our marriage the same way lightning comes from the clouds of the earth. Think of this as an early storm warning. Take a look overhead; are there dark clouds gathering? Can you hear the air beginning to crackle, and do you feel the hair standing up on the back of your neck? Then you'd better head for cover, because conflict is on its way. Any topic will do; that negative charge that fills the air has to go *somewhere*.

CLOUDS OF CONFUSION

Storm clouds gather in a marriage when there isn't time or effort made to spend time together to maintain a positive atmosphere. But dark clouds also gather because of conflict itself. Conflict is a mysterious and confusing process; once a conflict is under way, it can be incredibly difficult to sort out. Who started this? Whose fault is it? Who said what, and to whom? There are times when you can argue yourselves to a standstill, with no idea what to do or say next.

The authors of the book *Difficult Conversations* suggest that the reason conflicts are so confusing is that within every disagreement, there are really three conversations taking place at once:

1 *The "What Happened?" Conversation*
Who said what, and who did what?
Who's right, who meant what, and who's to blame?

2 *The Feelings Conversation*

Are my feelings valid? Appropriate? What do I do about the other person's feelings? What if he is angry or hurt?

3 *The Identity Conversation*

Am I competent or incompetent? Am I a good person or bad? Am I worthy of love or unlovable?

—*Adapted from* Difficult Conversations *by Stone, Patton, and Heen, 7–8*

We argue about the facts, but we don't seem to get anywhere; that's because the disagreement isn't really about facts at all but about the hurt feelings underneath. One spouse apologizes for criticizing the other, but it doesn't seem to help. That's because the argument is really about identity; a person feels incompetent when his spouse disapproves of him. A major conflict can create all the panic and confusion of a genuine thunderstorm.

If conflicts brew in the dark clouds that gather in our marriages, how can rules help? What good is a referee in a thunderstorm? When the wind is howling and lightning is flashing, that's when rules help most. In the perplexity of a storm, there's no telling what you'll do or say, and that only makes the conflict worse. Couples need to agree together on their emergency procedures before the big one hits. As we said before, success in conflict requires more than a set of rules. But rules can help bring order out of chaos, and when a storm is under way, chaos is the biggest enemy of all.

The Object of the GAME

"No, I don't know what we're fighting about.
Stop trying to distract me!"

THE OBJECT OF THE GAME

H*ave you ever watched the winter sport known as "curling"?*

The central piece of equipment is the curling stone, a forty-two-pound, disk-shaped block of granite with a handle glued to the top. The first contestant grabs the curling stone by the handle and slides it down the ice—did we mention this is played on ice? He must be careful to release the stone before he crosses the "hog line," which from the sound of it is probably a good thing to do. At this point, his teammates get involved; they hurry along in front of the stone, madly sweeping the ice with a broom made of horsehair.

And as you watch this Canadian national pastime, this recognized Olympic event, you ask yourself three questions:

1. Are they making this up as they go?
2. What in the world are they *doing*?
3. Why don't I have cable?

Every game has an object—even curling. As mysterious as the game may seem at first viewing, the competitors aren't doing all that work for nothing; they have a definite goal in mind. They may win, they may lose, but there *is* an object, and in any contest it is crucial to keep the object of the game clearly in mind.

The goal of billiards is not to see how far you can hit the ball. The goal of chess is not to advance to your opponent's side of the board and shout, "King me!" When you forget the object of the game, you work just as hard as everybody else, but you don't take home the prize—and you sometimes look pretty silly in the process.

When it comes to conflict, we all have a tendency to pursue the wrong object. Some of the most common mistaken objectives are:

- **To rationalize your actions**
- To prove yourself right

FIVE more mistaken objectives in a conflict

1
To change your spouse

2
To make him feel guilty or ashamed

3
To intimidate her into submission

4
To stir up a boring marriage

5
To prove that you know his motives

- **To prove your mate wrong**
- To punish the other person
- **To pay back for a previous offense**
- To vent anger

In the game of conflict, one erroneous objective reigns supreme: the desire to win the fight. Many marital conflicts are about nothing more than who will get the last word or who will get his way. But in marital conflict, victory is the prize that no one can afford to win.

Long ago, in ancient Greece, there lived a great general named Pyrrhus. His army once fought a major battle in his absence; a messenger brought Pyrrhus the news that, though his entire army had been wiped out, they had achieved a tactical victory. Pyrrhus responded, "A few more victories like that and Greece will be destroyed." Pyrrhus lent his name to a term we still use for a victory won at too great a price: a *Pyrrhic victory*.

That's exactly what victories are in marital conflict. You can overwhelm your mate with a barrage of accusations, you can jump from subject to subject until his head is spinning, or you can shout her into submissive silence. Victory! But as Pyrrhus would say, a few more victories like that and your marriage may be destroyed.

The old-time comic Jimmy Durante once described a fistfight he was involved in as a young man. "When I got through with that guy, he was covered with blood," he said. "*My* blood." When you achieve a marital victory, that blood you see is *your* blood—the blood of oneness, intimacy, and love.

Marriage is the only institution in the world where you can win every battle but lose the war. But if conflict is not about winning battles, what is it about? What is the true objective of the game that we need to keep in focus whenever the heat of battle begins to rage? There are three objectives that we must work to keep clearly in mind.

Objective 1:

To Understand Each Other Better

First Corinthians 14:33 says, "For God is not a God of confusion but of peace." This brief passage reminds us that the enemy of peace is *confusion,* which the dictionary defines as "a disturbed mental state." In an argument, couples often achieve a "disturbed mental state" due to undeniable differences between them in gender, temperament, values, and family background. That's why the first objective of the game of conflict is simply to understand each other better.

Peter encouraged husbands to "live with your wives in an understanding way" (1 Peter 3:7). His very words suggest a lifelong process, not a onetime event. After twenty years of marriage, some spouses assume that they know their partners inside and out. Who are they kidding? They may know all that they *care* to know, but the human heart is enormously complex and surprising. As Woody Allen put it, "'Know thyself'? I can't even find my way around Chinatown!"

Every conflict is a journey into the final frontier, and it helps to begin a trip with a destination in mind. The goal of the trip is to gather one more clue to help you understand the way your mate thinks, feels, and acts.

Objective 2:

To Develop Greater Intimacy

Conflict *is* a war of sorts—but it's not a war against your mate. It's a battle against the natural drift in every marriage toward coldness, distance, and isolation.

"The only thing necessary for the triumph of evil," wrote Edmund Burke, "is for good men to do nothing." Burke reminds us that, in a fallen world, evil has a momentum of its own. It needs no push to get it started; it's already under way, and unless we take steps to consciously resist it, evil will overtake us in a glacial advance. Marriage partners should remember Burke's words this way: "The only thing necessary for our marriage to become cold, angry, and loveless is for us to do nothing at all." In the busyness of life, when we make everything a priority but each other, this is easy to do.

Conflict is not a war *against* your mate but a battle *for* intimacy. Couples who adopt this mind-set become allies in a struggle against a common foe. We should try to enter every conflict with the attitude, "I am not willing to stay angry with you. I will not let us grow farther apart. I refuse to accept the coldness I feel growing between us." Every conflict is a fight, and few people enjoy fighting—but it's a lot more enjoyable to be fighting on the same side.

Objective 3:

To Clean Up Toxic Waste

When daily misunderstandings occur, they often leave behind a residue of anger, bitterness, or resentment. That residue can accumulate over time to create an environment toxic to oneness and intimacy. "Contentions are like the bars of a citadel," Proverbs reminds us (18:19). Our unaddressed grievances can become like prison bars that isolate us from one another and our common goals.

Conflict is like a toxic waste cleanup campaign, a concerted effort to collect and remove the junk and debris that separate us. We can't discuss every little difference between us, but when we make a regular habit of addressing our major grievances and resolving them in a peaceful way, that habit has a spillover effect. It tends to clear the air of a lot of other minor faults, flaws, and peccadilloes too.

If you're going to expend the energy to play the game, make sure your efforts contribute toward your goal. Remember, the hardest part of any task is simply to stay on track. When you play the game of conflict, keep these three objectives in mind.

INSIGHT
The goal in marriage is not to think alike but to think together.
—*Robert C. Dodds*

4

Why Play at ALL?

"I just want to say one more thing,
and then I'm going to run out of the room."

WHY PLAY AT ALL?

We have a friend who wrestled in the heavyweight division in college. During his senior year, he had an outstanding season and he qualified for the NCAA National Wrestling Championships. He won impressive victories in his preliminary rounds; he pinned and outpointed his opponents through the quarterfinals, then the semifinals . . . and then he lost the final round. The reason: His coach gave him the wrong time for the final match, and he showed up just in time to watch his rival accept the gold medal unchallenged. The moral of the story: To succeed at any event, it helps to show up for the game.

This principle may seem a bit obvious, but think about it. More conflicts are lost for one reason than any other: One partner did not care to show up.

There are different ways to "not show up," of course. Some spouses quickly change the subject to keep the conversation from going to unpleasant places. Some use humor or other forms of distraction to get their partner's mind on something else. Some immediately explode, like a peacock ruffling its tail feathers, hoping that the threat of escalation will stop the conflict in its tracks. Others stare off into space, or fold their arms and grit their teeth, or physically flee the room. . . . There are countless ways to not show up, and we all have our own favorite methods.

The initial motivation behind all this evasion is a good one: We want peace. We want peace more than conflict, quiet more than quarreling, and tidiness more than confusion. Who doesn't? But somewhere along the line our longing for tranquility takes a wrong turn,

---

---

and we find ourselves wanting peace more than oneness, quiet more than intimacy, and tidiness more than understanding.

But when we want peace more than oneness, we get neither. This is what C. S. Lewis called "the principle of first things." "Put first things first and we get second things thrown in," he wrote. "Put second things first and we lose *both* first and second things." Seek oneness more than peace, and you will find peace in the process; seek peace more than oneness, and you will lose them both.

The Word

He who separates himself seeks his own desire, he quarrels against all sound wisdom.

PROVERBS 18:1

Jesus emphasized the importance of nonavoidance in the gospel of Matthew. "This is how I want you to conduct yourself in these matters," He said. "If you enter your place of worship and, about to make an offering, you suddenly remember a grudge a friend has against you, abandon your offering, leave immediately, go to this friend and make things right. Then and only then, come back and work things out with God" (Matthew 5:23–24, THE MESSAGE). The "place of worship" in Jesus' example was the temple of Jerusalem, and a Jew wishing to make a sacrificial offering might have traveled hundreds of miles to get there. The trip involved considerable time, cost, and difficulty—even danger. Yet Jesus said that at the climactic moment, when the worshiper was standing before the altar itself, if he remembered that he had an unresolved conflict, he should drop everything. He should "go to this friend and make things right." He should put first things first. It's as though Jesus is reminding us, "I expect you to make conflict resolution a priority, and when you do, it will probably interrupt what you had planned. Peace comes at a price."

The most basic reason not to avoid conflict is simply that we re-

≡ **Foul!** ≡
To fail to initiate and engage emotionally with your wife will cause her to withdraw physically from you.

FIVE
things we use to
avoid interaction
with our mates

1
Work or career

2
TV

3
Hobbies, sports,
or activities

4
Children

5
Church involvement

INSIGHT
Some people use silence as a means of avoiding controversy or as a weapon to control, frustrate, or manipulate.... In the long run, silence never pays off. Even though the saying goes, "Silence is golden," it can also be yellow! Don't hide behind silence because you're afraid to deal with an issue.

—*H. Norman Wright in* Communication: Key to Your Marriage, *87–88*

INSIGHT

Handling conflicts functionally is rather like going to the dentist: You may find it a little (or even a lot!) painful for a while, but you're only making matters worse if you don't face the problem.

—*From* Interplay *by Adler, Rosenfeld, Towne, and Proctor, 392*

ally have no choice. If your mate has something she wants to say, and you demonstrate either verbally or nonverbally that you're unwilling to hear it, a conflict is already under way. It may not be the topic she originally intended, but it will do just fine, and now there are two conflicts woven together in a tangled, inseparable vine. The confusion of the original topic is now compounded by the new one: "Why won't you listen to me? Why don't you care? Why are you more concerned about your own comfort than the health of our marriage?" We call this scenario the "Credit Crunch." You can pay a little now, or a lot more later. But either way, you're going to pay.

INSIGHT

Only one feat is possible: not to have run away.

—*Dag Hammarskjöld*

To win at conflict, you have to show up for the game. No one enjoys conflict, but it's the shortsighted person who chooses to avoid it. Keep reading: When you learn to fight fair, you'll discover that conflict isn't nearly as bad as it used to be.

= Foul! =

One way we seek to avoid conflict is simply by keeping our interaction shallow.

INSIGHT

Never close your lips to those to whom you have opened your heart.

—*Charles Dickens*

Attitude Is EVERYTHING

"*I don't care. I still say it's just your opinion.*"

ATTITUDE IS EVERYTHING

SEVEN obstacles to resolving a conflict

1
ANGER

Many people don't want to give up their feelings of anger in order to forgive.

2
FEAR

Some people refuse to think about an incident that caused them great pain, much less focus on forgiving those who caused it.

3
PRIDE

Some people are too proud to admit that they have been hurt, since to them admitting hurt is admitting weakness or vulnerability.

4
BLACK-AND-WHITE THINKING

Some people firmly believe that it is foolish to believe that a person can change. They believe that once someone has hurt you, you can't trust that person.

(continued on page 37)

*M*any contests are won or lost before they even begin; it all has to do with the mind-set you bring to the game. Conflict is no different. It would be misleading for us to claim that success in conflict resolution all comes down to following a set of rules or being a good referee. The truth is, no set of rules will help you if you lack these six essential attitudes.

WILLINGNESS TO ENGAGE

The most important element in a game-winning attitude is a willingness to play the game at all. Don't take this attitude for granted; more is involved here than meets the eye.

Some people firmly believe that it is foolish to believe that a person can change. They believe that once someone has hurt you, you can't trust that person.

To "engage" means more than simply showing up. The word itself means "to involve oneself or become occupied; to become meshed or interlocked." It means to be willing to expend the energy necessary to wrestle through all the complexity and confusion of a conflict. It's what psychologist Tom Barrett calls "getting in the mud puddle" with your mate.

Are you willing to do what it takes to really resolve this issue, or do you just want to make it go away as quickly as possible?

Just showing up is better than nothing at all, but your mate can tell the difference between a begrudging, obligatory appearance and a wholehearted effort to listen and understand.

The Word

May the words of my mouth and the thoughts of my heart be pleasing to you, O Lord, my rock and my redeemer.

PSALM 19:14 NLT

HUMILITY

We often approach a conflict with the firm conviction that "I am absolutely right and my mate is completely wrong." The discussion that follows has a nasty habit of shattering that illusion.

An essential attitude in conflict resolution is the willingness to admit that you—yes, you, paragon of virtue that you are—just might be wrong, not just in this case but at any given moment. Conflicts become stubbornly entrenched when both spouses insist on attributing all the fault to their partner. Marital experience will teach you that perspectives can be remarkably different, and the sooner we become willing to admit that we probably played *some* role in the current disagreement, the sooner we'll be able to work toward resolution.

> **INSIGHT**
>
> **Lord, when we are wrong, make us willing to change, and when we are right, make us easy to live with.**
>
> —*Peter Marshall*

WILLINGNESS TO TAKE RESPONSIBILITY

If *humility* is the willingness to admit that you might be wrong, *responsibility* is the willingness to face the consequences of your actions. In marriage we are constantly being reminded of what we shouldn't have said, shouldn't have done, or shouldn't have forgotten. When the flaming finger of fault points to you, you have one of two choices: You can shift the blame to someone or something else, or you can take responsibility yourself.

The willingness to take responsibility is the dividing line between childhood and maturity. "We have not passed that subtle line between childhood and adulthood," writes Sydney J. Harris, "until we have stopped saying 'It got lost,' and say, 'I lost it.'"

WILLINGNESS TO CHANGE

With age comes a phenomenon known as "hardening of the attitudes." We speak of people becoming "set in their ways," as though, like curing concrete, they have thickened and toughened and ceased

---

5
UNREASONABLE EXPECTATIONS OF OTHERS
In order to forgive, we must understand that we all make mistakes, we all fall short of our potential, and we all have a dark side.

6
SITTING IN JUDGMENT
Perhaps the biggest obstacle to forgiveness is our tendency to judge others harshly.

7
LACK OF EMPATHY
In order for some of us to gain empathy for wrongdoers, we need to admit to ourselves that we have been guilty of committing the same or a similar offense.

—*Adapted from* The Power of Apology *by Beverly Engel,* 88–101

INSIGHT
It is human to err, but it is devilish to remain willfully in error.
—*Saint Augustine*

FOUR
tests of true humility

1

A nondefensive spirit when confronted

2

A willingness to be accountable

3

An attitude of "Nothing to prove, nothing to lose"

4

An authentic desire to help others

—*Adapted from*
Improving Your Serve
by Charles Swindoll, 25

INSIGHT

Often we change jobs, friends, and spouses instead of ourselves.

—*Akbarali H. Jetha*

INSIGHT

Laughter is the shortest distance between two people.

—*Victor Borge*

TIP

ASK YOUR MATE, "WHAT WOULD YOU LIKE ME TO CHANGE?"

---

to adapt. But change is a part of life, and a willingness to change is a vital attitude in marriage.

Francis Bacon once wrote, "He that will not apply new remedies must expect new evils." Those "new evils" might include recurring arguments, growing bitterness, and a mate who suspects you of arrogance and inflexibility. There are bountiful dividends from assuming an attitude that says to your mate, "I'm willing to change anything that will give us a better life together."

SENSE OF HUMOR

Whoever said, "There is a fine line between tragedy and comedy" must have been married. It's a wise person who is able to spot the humor in all the strangeness and confusion of relationships.

A sense of humor has to be seasoned with humility. That means the starting point of all humor is the ability to laugh at yourself, not your mate. Anyone can laugh at someone else's foibles; that may be nothing more than arrogance or indifference. Humility is contagious, and the way to cultivate a sense of humor in your home is by demonstrating the ability to laugh at your own weirdness, pomposity, and eccentricity.

A THICK SKIN

In a crowd, it's impossible to avoid getting our toes stepped on— and nothing is as crowded as a busy family. It's inevitable that we'll get our feelings hurt from time to time, and that's why there's no more valuable asset than a thick skin.

A "thick skin" is simply the ability to let things go. In marriage we all need the wisdom to know the difference between a serious offense and a minor faux pas. Treating every slight or snub as a conflict requiring discussion and resolution would be

INSIGHT

All the water in all the oceans cannot sink a ship unless it gets inside.

—*Eugene Peterson*

exhausting. Some things we simply have to overlook—and we have to be able to overlook them without bitterness or resentment.

Conflict is often a game played without rules. More important, conflict is often a game played with a losing attitude. These are the attitudes that are crucial to winning at conflict. If you have them, you'll find that the rules seem less necessary; without them, no number of rules will take their place. For more help with discovering a winning attitude, see Appendix B: Attitude Is Everything.

The SETUP

"One thing before you go to sleep: Name all the women you knew before me."

THE SETUP

The FIVE worst places to try to resolve a conflict

1
In front of the TV

2
In front of the kids

3
In public

4
In transit

5
From different rooms

Every game involves some kind of setup. Football requires chalk lines and benches; Monopoly requires a playing board, property cards, and dice. A productive conflict requires a kind of setup too: thoughtful consideration of the time and place the game is to be played. Here are three steps to setting up the game properly.

THE PLAYING BOARD

Every conflict takes place on a playing board—the environment where the disagreement occurs. Many a conflict is doomed from the start by a poor choice of settings. We once attended a marriage seminar where the couples were all sent to a hotel sports bar to discuss their relationships. On every wall, just above each woman's shoulder, was a flat-panel TV presenting a different football game. Imagine the intimate connections!

Each of us has best and worst places to try to have a serious discussion. Some people are multitaskers and have no trouble holding a conversation in front of a blaring television. For others, it would be impossible to concentrate in an environment like that. There is no single playing board for conflict; the goal is to find the places that work best for you.

Now let's be reasonable. For some of us, the ideal place to host an intimate discussion is in the shade of a palm tree on a white-sanded beach in Puerto Vallarta. Welcome to reality; that's not going to happen. The fact is, we almost always hold our discussions in less-than-perfect environments, complete with demanding doorbells, ringing telephones, and

> **TIP**
> IF YOU'RE EASILY DISTRACTED, WHEN YOU SIT TOGETHER AT A RESTAURANT, CHOOSE A SEAT THAT DOESN'T FACE THE ENTRANCE OR A TV.

howling children. The trick is to pick the best *available* environment and then anticipate and eliminate as many distractions as possible.

Understanding the opposite sex is difficult enough; why make your environment work against you? The next time a disagreement begins to surface, you might consider saying, "I don't think this is a good place to discuss this. Can we try it over there?"

GAME TIME

Just as there are good and bad environments for conflict, there are good and bad times too. Sometimes we destine a discussion for failure by beginning at an inopportune moment or without enough time to complete the dialogue. There's nothing more frustrating than opening a wound, only to have to leave it festering for hours (or days) until you have time to tend to it again.

Once again, let's be realistic. There are very few ideal times for a disagreement: times when you are both rested, focused, and motivated to work together. Unfortunately, the times that are best for a conflict are also great times for golf, or reading, or sex—everything *but* conflict. We have to remember the priority of resolving our disagreements and devote some of our better times to it. That may sound painful, but it's ultimately a time-saver. Conflicts that are launched at poorly chosen moments often take longer to resolve, because the timing (or the lack of timing) becomes part of the disagreement itself.

For some of us, there seem to be no good times or places for conflict. We can *always* think of something better to do. But it does no good to say to our mate, "I really can't discuss problems in North America, or on days that end in 'y.'" That's just using setup as an excuse for avoidance. If the time and place of a

> **The Word**
> The heart of the righteous ponders how to answer, but the mouth of the wicked pours out evil things.
> PROVERBS 15:28

> **The FIVE worst times to try to resolve a conflict**
>
> **1**
> Just before sleep
>
> **2**
> Just before intimacy
>
> **3**
> On the way to church
>
> **4**
> When you're leaving for work
>
> **5**
> When you've just stepped in the door
>
> *TIP*—GENERATE YOUR OWN AGREED-UPON LIST OF BEST TIMES AND PLACES FOR SERIOUS DISCUSSIONS.

> **INSIGHT**
> Good communication is as stimulating as black coffee, and just as hard to sleep after.
> —*Anne Morrow Lindbergh*

disagreement are unacceptable to you, then it's *your* responsibility to suggest a better one. It's not enough to say, "I can't talk about this now." You need to also say, "Tonight, when the kids are in bed, would be much better."

INSIGHT
Nobody stands
taller than those
willing to stand
corrected.
—William Safire

THE BEGINNING OF THE GAME

Most games seem to take a slow, rolling start. That's a good way to avoid early errors and pulled hamstrings. Conflict requires a cautious approach as well. Sometimes our biggest mistakes occur in our over-zealousness to jump right in and get things resolved. "Fools rush in," the old saying goes, but angels fear to tread on other people's feelings, fears, and frailties.

Marital researcher John Gottman claims that the start-up of an argument is a crucial time, because arguments tend to end the same way they begin. Angry beginnings lead to angry conclusions, and gracious beginnings lead to gracious resolutions. All the more reason to consider carefully before charging ahead into a conflict.

❗Just a reminder to turn to the appendix where you can create your own rules for fighting fair based on what you've found helpful in this chapter.

The INNER GAME of Conflict

When women REALLY make eye contact

THE INNER GAME OF CONFLICT

W. *Timothy Galwey begins his book* The Inner Game of Tennis *with these words: "The problems that most perplex tennis players are not those dealing with the proper way to swing a racket. Books and professionals giving this information abound. Nor do most players complain excessively about their physical limitations. The most common complaint of sportsmen ringing down the corridors of the ages is, 'It's not that I don't know what to do, it's that I don't do what I know!'"*

INSIGHT

Be not angry that you cannot make others as you wish to be, since you cannot make yourself as you wish to be.

—*Thomas à Kempis*

The same is true of the game of conflict. In many cases, it's not that we don't know what to do—we just have a hard time doing it. Why are our disagreements sometimes so puzzling and perplexing? At times you may find yourself staring at your mate and thinking, *What in the world are you talking about? Come to think of it, what am I talking about?*

Galwey says that when it comes to tennis, there is an inner game that has to be addressed before the outer game can be mastered. So, too, with conflict. We begin to address the inner game of conflict once we recognize that *conflict is essentially a spiritual activity.*

In the book of Ephesians the apostle Paul reminds us: "For we are not fighting against people made of flesh and blood, but against the evil rulers and authorities of the unseen world, against those mighty powers of darkness who rule this world, and against wicked spirits in the heavenly realms"

INSIGHT

Any concern too small to be turned into a prayer is too small to be made into a burden.

—*Corrie ten Boom*

(Ephesians 6:12 NLT). We could paraphrase his words this way: "When you have a fight with your mate, more is going on than meets the eye. There is a struggle going on at a much deeper level. Your disagreement is just the tip of an iceberg."

Like all icebergs, the greatest danger comes from the ice that lurks below the waterline. That's why it pays to address the *inner* game of conflict before the outer game begins. One of the most practical, productive approaches to any conflict is to make a habit of praying before you begin. We've found that taking just a few moments to pray together provides four crucial advantages.

UNDERSTANDING

Jesus once complained about a lack of understanding on the part of His listeners. "'For the hearts of these people are hardened,'" He said, "'and their ears cannot hear, and they have closed their eyes—so their eyes cannot see, and their ears cannot hear, and their hearts cannot understand'" (Matthew 13:15 NLT). Jesus' listeners were not blind and deaf; they had a heart condition that made understanding impossible. In our own conflicts we sometimes suffer the same affliction. Words abound, in sufficient quantity and *more* than ample volume, but no one seems to understand.

Proverbs 20:12 says, "The hearing ear and the seeing eye, the Lord has made both of them." Almost everyone is born with physical eyes and ears—but eyes that can see and ears that will hear are another matter. Understanding, we are told, is a spiritual issue. A wise person asks for help in sorting through all the befuddling complexities of a disagreement.

> *TIP*—ASK GOD FOR THE WISDOM TO KNOW WHEN TO BE SILENT AS WELL.

WISDOM

Wisdom is knowing what to do and say next. James reminds us, "If any of you lacks wisdom, let him ask of God, who gives to all generously and without reproach, and it will be given to him" (James 1:5). We all tend to lack wisdom in a heated argument, and we could all use some guidance in selecting that all-important next word or phrase. "The answer of the tongue is from the Lord," Proverbs reminds us (16:1), so we might as well seek that answer from its Source.

INSIGHT

Most of us don't feel like praying with someone we are having a disagreement with. But inviting the Prince of Peace into our boat in the middle of the storm is truly the answer.

—*From* Two Hearts Praying as One *by Dennis and Barbara Rainey, 29–30*

ACCOUNTABILITY

John 3:20 says, "Everyone who does evil hates the Light, and does not come to the Light for fear that his deeds will be exposed." There's nothing like the prospect of praying together to encourage a couple to keep short accounts. It's awfully convicting to treat your mate with disrespect or contempt and then to have to drag those dirty deeds into the revealing spotlight of prayer. Maybe that's why counselors say that when chronic conflict sets in, praying together is one of the first things to go.

And that's why we should make a commitment to do it. Praying before a conflict has a way of gen-erating humility, contrition, and generosity—qualities that serve us well in reaching a peaceful agreement. Try pulling up an empty chair and setting it across from you as a visual reminder that there is a third party attending your disagreement. You'll find that reminder tends to produce civility the same way a houseguest tends to improve manners.

TIP

TRY HOLDING HANDS WHEN YOU PRAY. IT'S A GREAT WAY TO DEFUSE ANGER AND COMMUNICATE WARMTH WITHOUT WORDS.

The Word

I am the Vine, you are the branches. When you're joined with me and I with you, the relation intimate and organic, the harvest is sure to be abundant. Separated, you can't produce a thing.

JOHN 15:5 THE MESSAGE

PEACE

In the last chapter we reminded you of John Gottman's words: "The research shows that if your discussion begins with a harsh start-up, it will inevitably end on a negative note, even if there are a lot of attempts to 'make nice' in between." Praying together helps to avoid harsh start-ups by lowering the emotional note on which a conflict begins. Quiet, calm, and respect are all mental at-titudes that we bring to prayer, and that mind-set may be a big improve-ment over the attitude you had just a few minutes ago.

The Word

The one who knows much says little; an understanding person remains calm.

PROVERBS 17:27 THE MESSAGE

What would a prefight prayer sound like? We recommend something like this:

Lord, we know that You have graciously forgiven us for the things that we have done wrong. Help us to remember that and to generously share that forgiveness with each other. Help us to understand each other; give us kind, gentle, and gracious words; help us to remember Your presence here and to speak and act accordingly. Give us humility, control our anger, and leave us with a greater love for each other when our conversation is done.

When a conflict is about to begin, praying together may be the last thing we think to do. But when we develop this habit, we begin to address the inner game of conflict—and that may be where the game is really won or lost.

INSIGHT

Nothing lowers the level of conversation more than raising the voice.

—*Stanley Horowitz*

≡ Foul! ≡

Pray for your own weaknesses and shortcomings, not just your mate's: "Lord, I agree with Mary that she needs to be more kind. . . ."

OUT with the Old RULES

DOWNS

"Do you really want to go into all this, or would you rather just apologize now?"

OUT WITH THE OLD RULES

If you're reading this book, then you're probably not a newcomer to the game of conflict. No one is, really. You've been honing your skills of negotiation and compromise since the day you gave your brother a black eye and he threatened to tell your mom. Over the years we've all developed an instinctive strategy of conflict that guides our disagreements even to this day.

And that's the problem. Because conflict is a game without rules, we've also collected some bad habits in our approach to this game. Old habits are hard to break—and old, bad habits are the hardest of all. Here are five questions that will let you identify your unproductive approaches to conflict and help make way for new ones.

WHAT IS YOUR NATURAL STYLE OF CONFLICT?

According to communication scholars, there are five basic styles of conflict:

1 **Nonassertive.** This person is unable or unwilling to express her thoughts and feelings. Her instinct is to avoid a conflict altogether, or to simply give in to her partner's demands in order to put an end to the disagreement as quickly as possible: "OK, fine, I'm sorry; I blew it. Whatever. Do we really need to go into all this?"

Some women think that this is what submission means—to go along with their husbands without giving input. This is the easy way out and is not God's intention. Our husbands need our thoughts and insights, and they are to respect and value them.

Men sometimes think that by stating their case loudly or with authority they can intimidate their wives into thinking as they do. This will only cause resentment and disrespect.

⚌ Foul! ⚌

Don't say, "Uh-huh," "Right," or "I agree" just to pacify your mate if you have no real intention of addressing the problem or doing what she's asking you to do. You need to discuss it further.

2 **Directly aggressive.** This person lashes out through attacks on his partner's character, competence, or appearance. He may resort to ridicule, threats, shouting, or swearing to overpower his partner and get his way: "That's just stupid! You're too easy on the kids, and you're a lousy mother."

3 **Passive-aggressive.** The passive-aggressive person expresses her hostility in a disguised, underhanded manner to undermine and frustrate her partner's wishes. When challenged on her actions, she will deny any wrongdoing: "Did that make you angry? Oh, I'm sorry. I had no idea that you'd be so sensitive about it. . . ."

4 **Indirect.** This person prefers to convey messages through hinting, sarcasm, humor, or nonverbal expressions like a heavy sigh. The goal is to minimize the risk of open confrontation or rejection: "It would be nice to have a little help around here, not that anyone cares. . . ."

5 **Assertive.** This person attempts to express her thoughts and feelings clearly and directly to her partner, and she allows him to express his views the same way in return: "Do you have a minute? Something is bothering me, and I'd like to talk it over with you."

The fifth style of conflict, *assertive*, is by far the most productive. Don't confuse "assertive" with "aggressive." *Assertive* means bold or confident, while *aggressive* implies harshness or hostility. The assertive communicator is not blunt, rude, or uncaring; she is simply bold about engaging her partner and seeking a resolution that will satisfy them both.

> **═ Foul! ═**
>
> Since a woman tends to pick up nonverbal cues quickly, she often assumes that her husband does too—but he often doesn't. Don't be indirect, expect him to connect the dots, and then become angry with him when he doesn't.

Which approach to conflict sounds most like your instinctive style? The *reason* for your style of conflict may be found in your answer to the next question. . . .

HOW WAS CONFLICT HANDLED IN YOUR FAMILY OF ORIGIN?

We know a husband and wife who grew up in two very different families. In her family, the dinner table was like a sanctuary, a place of peace where no unkind word was ever spoken. But in his family, the dinner table was more like a WWF Smackdown. Debating, deriding, and aggressively interrupting were all just family fun. Her first dinner at his house was a devastating experience. *What did I do wrong?* she kept asking herself. *Why are these people so mad at me?*

Some of our families dealt with their disagreements openly and constructively, and as a result we've come to see conflict for what it is: a natural part of relationships and a skill that has to be learned. In other families, conflict was strictly forbidden; disagreement was never appropriate, and the first hint of hostility or division brought a rapid response from Mom and Dad. If this was your family, then conflict for you may seem like a caged beast. Do you dare let it out of the cage? What would happen if you do? For still others, family conflict was an ugly and painful experience, and if that was your experience, conflict is probably something you want to avoid at all costs.

How was conflict handled in *your* family? Your answer to that question may explain your response to the next one. . . .

WHAT DOES CONFLICT MEAN TO YOU?

This is a question to consider on a gut level: What does it feel like, deep down inside, when you begin to have a heated disagreement with the one you love most in all the world? Does it feel like failure? Do you

---

TIP

ASK YOURSELF, "DID PEOPLE IN MY FAMILY OF ORIGIN APOLOGIZE TO ONE ANOTHER? WAS I EVER TAUGHT HOW TO APOLOGIZE? DID MY PARENTS EVER APOLOGIZE TO ME?"

INSIGHT

If you can accept and profit by criticism, you have a priceless ability possessed by few of your fellowmen.

—*Former Chief Justice Charles Evans Hughes*

feel rejected? Do you fear the loss of your mate's love or respect? Do you feel frightened, insecure, or in danger?

Conflict means different things to different people, from a major threat to a minor annoyance to business as usual. What conflict *means* to you will influence the way you tend to go about it.

WHAT ARE YOUR CONFLICT RITUALS?

Conflict rituals are habitual patterns of behavior that we slip into whenever a disagreement arises. At some time in the distant past, we tried this approach and it seemed to work; now the approach has become our standard procedure, a kind of ritual we enact to deal with conflicts of all shapes and sizes. It may no longer work; it may have ceased to work years ago; but as we said before, old habits are hard to break.

Consider a couple of common conflict rituals:

She: Brings up a complaint or concern.
He: Feels blamed, begins to shut down and withdraw.
She: Becomes increasingly forceful and aggressive.
He: Charges out. He returns later with a gift but no apology or explanation.
They: Move on as if the conflict never happened.

He: Brings up a complaint or concern.
She: Instantly counters with an issue of her own.
He: Responds to her concern with yet another complaint.
They: Continue to rapidly introduce more and more topics until further discussion is impossible. They overload and shut down in frustration.

But these approaches to conflict are so *obviously* unproductive. Why would anyone do what he knows won't work? It's human nature; when faced with the baffling or mysterious, we resort to the familiar— even when it doesn't help.

What are your conflict rituals? What are the familiar approaches you instinctively use to make sense of the bewildering? What old habits are keeping you from making real headway in resolving differences with your mate?

WHAT ARE YOU REALLY FIGHTING ABOUT?

Nothing can keep an argument going like two people who aren't sure what they're arguing about. If you find yourselves revisiting the same topic again and again, the problem may not be one of style but substance. It's hard to resolve a disagreement until you're able to identify the real issue. Until you do, you're dealing only with symptoms and not the real disease.

In our first book, *One of Us Must Be Crazy . . . And I'm Pretty Sure It's You*, we identified seven underlying issues that are the root cause of most of the conflict in married life. **Couples sometimes spend years in conflict over a specific topic, only to discover that all along they have really been fighting about something else. For example:**

WHEN YOU DISAGREE ABOUT	YOU MAY REALLY BE ARGUING ABOUT
Saving vs. spending, parenting differences	SECURITY
In-law disputes, looking at the opposite sex	LOYALTY
Lending time and money, obeying traffic laws	RESPONSIBILITY
Passivity, avoiding disagreements	CARING
Household chores, planning ahead	ORDER
Social activities, use of leisure time	OPENNESS
Decision making, communication	CONNECTION

Stop wasting time and energy over superficial topics; get down to the fundamental issues that separate you. Make an effort to understand these seven areas of conflict, and spend your time talking about what really matters.

Take a few minutes to peruse these five questions. What are your old rules? In the "Our Rules" section at the back of the book, write down some things that just don't work for you—then let's talk about some things that do.

Just a reminder to turn to the appendix where you can create your own rules for fighting fair based on what you've found helpful in this chapter.

9

Passing the Dice

"But if I don't finish your sentences for you,
they won't come out the way I want them to."

PASSING THE DICE

*P*ick out a board game—any game will do. Now take off the lid, turn it over, and search for these words: "Roll the dice to see who goes first. Play proceeds clockwise. . . ." All games include directions to make sure everyone knows whose turn it is. But conflict, as you recall, is a game without rules. In a disagreement it isn't always easy to know who goes first, who comes next, and who just got left out.

INSIGHT

If we could read the secret history of our enemies, we should find in each person's life sorrow and suffering enough to disarm all hostility.

—Henry Wadsworth Longfellow

There's a simple set of instructions that can help create order out of this chaos. In the game of conflict, the order of play goes like this: Listen long; then speak short—and don't forget to pass the dice.

Sounds easy, doesn't it? It's not. *How* you listen and *how* you speak makes all the difference. When you do it right, the game proceeds nicely and both of you get to play; when you do it wrong, each of you thinks it's his turn and both players are scrambling for the dice.

The Word
A fool does not delight in understanding, but only in revealing his own mind.
PROVERBS 18:2

More than anything else, anger begins because of errors in the way we listen and express ourselves. Not in what we hear but in what we *think* we hear; not in what we say but in *how* we say it.

Here are some helpful suggestions to improve the order of play in your next disagreement.

LISTEN UP!

James 1:19 gives us a simple order of priority for communication. "Everyone must be quick to hear, slow to speak and slow to anger." In James's perspective we make two common errors in a conflict: We speak too soon, and we get mad too fast. *Slow it down,* he says—but there's one thing that definitely needs to shift to a higher gear: our listening.

We tend to think of listening in a passive sense—as something that happens *to* us, like tasting or feeling. We don't have to do anything; it just happens. Not so. Listening is an active skill, and there are things we can do to become more skillful listeners.

LISTEN WITH EVERYTHING YOU'VE GOT.

Someone once said that a good definition of "eternity" is to listen to a five-year-old recount the plot of this neat movie he saw. Every parent knows that listening—*real* listening—is hard work. It requires energy, focus, and endurance—things that are always in short supply. But every parent will also tell you that listening is some of the most important work a parent can do.

> **INSIGHT**
>
> **Before marriage, a man will lie awake all night thinking about something you said; after marriage, he'll fall asleep before you finish saying it.**
>
> —*Helen Rowland*

No one loves hard labor, and it's only human nature to look for short-cuts. When it comes to listening, we've all learned dozens of ways to look like we're listening while our mind is really picking flowers somewhere else. You're a master of the out-of-body experience, and your mate knows how to recognize it. There are telltale signs: Your eyes glaze over like a walleyed pike, or you begin to hum the theme song from your favorite TV show, or you start feeling around for the remote. When you do, you might as well strap on a flashing neon sign that screams, "I DON'T CARE!"

When you have real work to do, you buckle down and do it. No distractions, no interruptions—you've got work to do. We need to treat the work of listening the same way. The next time you've got some listening to do, turn off the TV. Scoot forward and sit on the edge of the sofa. Lock eyes with your partner like a tractor beam and refuse to look away. And when you find your mind occasionally drifting off to

----

INSIGHT— **The greatest gift you can give another is the purity of your attention.** —*Richard Moss, M.D.*

SIX benefits of silence

1
It makes room for
LISTENING.

2
It gives us freedom to
OBSERVE.

3
It allows time to
THINK.

4
It provides space in
which to **FEEL.**

5
It lets us broaden our
AWARENESS.

6
It opens us to the entry
of **PEACE.**

Author Unknown

TIP—DON'T SAY "UH-HUH" WHEN YOU'RE NOT REALLY LISTENING. SAY "JUST A MINUTE" INSTEAD.

the putting green, make a practice of saying, "Hold it. I missed what you said. Would you repeat that last sentence?"

If you'll do these things, even when you and your mate disagree, you'll find that you still get bonus points for caring and for trying—and a few extra points can make all the difference.

LISTEN WITH AN OPEN MIND.

We sometimes listen only for the points that confirm what we already believe. That means we approach a discussion with a lot of assumptions—about the way our mate thinks, what he really wants, and why he acts the way he does. Sometimes our assumptions are so stubbornly entrenched that we're unwilling to consider any thoughts to the contrary. We hear only what we want to hear, and our partner's words are like a rock skipping across our mental pond, making contact only at preselected points.

Your mate wants to be thought of as a human being, not as a predictable formula. The next time you and your mate have a discussion, try to imagine that you are looking at a perfect stranger wearing a mask of your mate. Expect to hear something new, something that doesn't fit with what you already know. Tell yourself that you are engaging in a cross-cultural experience—because, in point of fact, that's exactly what marriage is. You'll find that a simple change of attitude can help you to listen with an open mind.

LISTEN WITH YOUR HEART, NOT JUST YOUR HEAD.

Some of us listen like court reporters, staring stone-faced at our partner while we dutifully record her comments. We listen like students in a boring classroom lecture—but she isn't giving a lecture; she's sharing her heart. She wants to know more than if you got the words right; she wants to know if you got the feeling *behind* the words. That's why it helps to listen *reflexively*—that means to think of listening as a two-way street. Nod your head, give a sympathetic sigh, or throw in a little "Wow!" or "Really?" from time to time—anything to let her know that there's still someone on the other end of the line, and that you not only hear her words but feel them too.

LISTEN TO WHAT *ISN'T* BEING SAID.

Communication scholars talk about *high-* and *low-context* relationships. In a low-context relationship, we count on words to do the talking for us, and we use them freely and directly. The American culture as a whole is a low-context culture; when a group of Americans gathers for a meeting and someone leaves the door open, we simply say, "Close the door."

But the Japanese culture is traditionally high-context. Japanese count on the context *surrounding* the words to help get the message across: gestures, facial expressions, and minute variations in tone of voice. They communicate more indirectly, often through hints and suggestions, and they expect one another to understand what is meant when someone says, "It would be nice if the door were shut."

There are high- and low-context communicators in marriage, too. Low-context partners are *verbal* communicators; they say what they mean and mean what they say, and they depend on words to carry the message. Their motto is, "If you want to know what I mean, listen to what I say."

But for high-context spouses, that level of directness feels so blunt, so demanding, so *obvious*. They prefer to let out a sigh, or roll their eyes, or drop a little hint. High-context partners use words too, but they're also *nonverbal* communicators. Their dictum: "If you want to know what I mean, watch everything I do."

When nonverbal spouses listen to their verbal partners, they have a tendency to *read into* what's being said. *Why did he say it like that? Why was he standing that way? Why did he drop his voice just then?* Nonverbal listeners are skilled at finding the message *behind* the words—even when there isn't one there.

But verbal listeners have the opposite problem. Because of their preference for words, they often overlook much of what their mate is trying to communicate by ignoring her body language, tone of voice, and facial

How to ignore someone's advice without causing hurt feelings

1
Show appreciation for the input.

2
Give two reasons why you agree and one reason why you don't.

3
Thank her for getting you thinking.

4
Seek out her opinion on something else.

From Make Peace with Anyone *by David Lieberman, 27–28*

≡ Foul! ≡

Folding your arms, rolling your eyes, shaking your head, sighing deeply, looking at the clock, or leaning toward the door.

THREE overlooked forms of nonverbal communication

1
DISTANCE
Don't let physical distance create emotional separation. Sit or stand close enough to have a personal conversation.

2
ORIENTATION
Don't try to have a conversation facing in opposite directions. If face-to-face feels too confrontational, then sit side by side.

3
PHYSICAL CONTACT
Touch is a form of communication too. Many couples find that it helps to touch or even hold hands when they talk.

expressions. "But that's not what you *said*. What you *said* is . . ."

Sometimes the meat of a message comes through everything *but* the words. If you want to become a more skillful listener, try lending an ear to what *isn't* being said.

LISTEN UNTIL *SHE'S* SATISFIED.

We tend to listen only until we understand, or until it sounds familiar, or until we decide what to say next. We tend to listen only until *we're* satisfied—but this isn't about you. She's the one who's speaking now, and you need to let her talk until she's said what she wants to say in the way she wants to say it.

Remember, conflict is not only about facts but feelings. We don't just want to be listened to; we want to *feel heard,* and that takes time. It means we all need to become more leisurely listeners. If you listen only until you've got the facts, you may have missed entirely what she really wants to say.

TIP
WANT TO KNOW IF SHE'S SATISFIED? ASK, "DO YOU FEEL LIKE I REALLY HEARD YOU?"

SPEAK UP!

The human tongue has been called "the world's deadliest blunt instrument." The book of Proverbs agrees: "Death and life are in the power of the tongue," it warns us, "and those who love it will eat its fruit" (18:21). We could add a corollary: "And those who abuse it will suffer the consequences." Our words have the power to heal and to destroy; they have the power to make peace out of war, or to turn a minor difference of opinion into a lifelong blood feud.

Here are five ways to turn the world's deadliest blunt instrument into an implement of healing and compassion.

BE A MAN OF FEW WORDS.

The book of Proverbs warns us against the use of five types of words that have the power to wound our mates—the sort of words that abound when a conflict picks up speed and anger clouds our better judgment.

- **RASH WORDS**
- HARSH WORDS
- **BACKBITING WORDS**
- EMPTY WORDS
- **MANY WORDS**

Notice that final category: *many* words. As Proverbs puts it, "When there are many words, transgression is unavoidable, but he who restrains his lips is wise" (10:19). Be careful with this principle: This is not an excuse to shut down, clam up, and avoid conflict. More than anything, it's a reminder to simply slow down and think carefully before you speak. Unlike automobiles, words cannot be recalled to the factory for adjustment. Once they roll off the tongue, the damage is done, and you may find yourself doing cleanup for quite a while.

When the pace of a conflict begins to accelerate, watch out; when the words start to fly, someone's going to get hurt. Take a breath, take a break, and make sure the words you *use* are the words you *choose*.

INSIGHT

Spilling your guts is just exactly as charming as it sounds.

—*Fran Lebowitz*

SAY IT AGAIN, SAM.

Words are deceptively simple objects. The little word *run* has twenty-six different definitions in the dictionary! There's nothing easier than stringing words together in a sentence, but there's nothing more difficult than making sense of what someone else has said.

Communication is something like mixing paint on a palette. You start with red on one side and blue on the other; somewhere in the middle, when they blend together, you get purple. In communication, you have a speaker on one side and a listener on the other; somewhere

----

TIP—EXTROVERTS MAY NEED TO PAY SPECIAL ATTENTION. THEY TEND TO THINK FAST AND SPEAK AS THEY THINK. INTROVERTS HAVE AN ADVANTAGE HERE; THEY MORE NATURALLY WEIGH THEIR WORDS BEFORE UTTERING THEM.

SIX ways for a man to listen to his wife

1
Lean forward and look into her eyes.

2
Inquire by saying, "Tell me more."

3
Stop interrupting with your "answers."

4
Tell her what you heard her say and ask if you are right.

5
Express comfort: "I am so sorry for how you have suffered."

6
Never look at your watch while she is talking.

Adapted from Covenant Marriage *by Fred Lowery*

EIGHT
ways to help
your husband
hear you

1. Use "would," not "could," when asking a man to do something. Women use "could" because it seems more polite, but men prefer the direct approach.

2. Say what you think. Don't give clues—even big ones—and expect him to grab on to them and read your mind.

3. Be concise and to the point. Spare him the details unless he's a detail-loving man, which would be quite rare.

4. When asking for his input, make certain you understand what he means. If you don't, ask until you do.

5. Don't accuse him of not listening to you. Keep your story short, and assume that he's listening.

6. Realize that women place a higher value on listening than most men do. To a woman, it's another way of expressing love; to a man it's more like a task.

7. Thank him when he has listened to you. Help your husband feel more confident by noticing and praising his efforts.

8. Share with others (when he can hear you) what a great listener he is. He'll feel fabulous, and before long he'll begin to think of himself as a good listener as well.

Adapted from How to Get Your Husband to Talk to You *by Nancy Cobb and Connie Grigsby, 156–57*

The Word
Be gracious in your speech. The goal is to bring out the best in others in a conversation, not put them down, not cut them out.

COLOSSIANS 4:6
THE MESSAGE

in the middle, when everything works just right, you get *meaning*.

Sometimes you express yourself in words that—to *you*—have absolute, crystalline clarity. You construct a masterful sentence, a model of good communication, a virtual string of pearls—yet somehow, your mate has no idea what you're talking about. When that happens, you want to put all the blame on him. He isn't listening, or he isn't concentrating, or he's just being deliberately thickheaded. Maybe—but just maybe your meaning got lost in that dark expanse between speaking and listening.

When that happens, say it again. Don't just repeat yourself, insisting that any child should be able to understand. Say it a different way, and if necessary, say it another way still. Be patient. Remind yourself that *meaning* is a mysterious business, and resist the temptation to blame the whole problem on your mate's bad attitude. He may be more than willing to understand; he may just need to hear it put a different way.

SPEAK TO HEAL, NOT TO WOUND.

As powerful as words are, we treat them with casual disregard. "There is one who speaks rashly like the thrusts of a sword," Proverbs says (12:18). If we treated knives the way we treat words, there would be bodies everywhere. If Proverbs is correct about the power of the tongue, then we all carry a concealed weapon—without a permit, without training, and without restraint.

A concise summary of the Bible's teaching on speech can be found in Ephesians 4:29: "Don't use foul or abusive language. Let everything you say be good and helpful, so that your words will be an encouragement to those who hear them" (NLT). This summary can be further reduced to a single, memorable

> **Foul!**
> Sometimes we wound our mates the deepest not through direct attack, but through sarcasm, insult, and innuendo.

principle: "Speak to heal, not to harm."

This is what we like to call "the Healing Word." That means that, in addition to the concealed weapon you carry, you also carry about with you the power to heal. Have you ever daydreamed about being a famous surgeon with a great gift of healing? You have that gift, in the power of your tongue. Care to try it out? Think about your mate for a minute. . . . Think of one thing you could say to him that would make him feel admired, encouraged, or appreciated. The next time you see him, try it out. You can actually see healing take place before your eyes.

In your next disagreement, when the weapons are drawn and the bullets are starting to fly, apply the power of the Healing Word. Everyone knows how to tear down; what is the one thing you could say that might help put the guns away and begin to bring healing to the conflict?

BEGIN AN UPWARD SPIRAL.

Communication scholars describe a phenomenon known as a "communication spiral," a situation where the mood, pace, and volume of a conversation are going downhill fast. But communication spirals go in both directions; if the downward momentum can be halted, the direction can be reversed; then an "upward spiral" is under way.

An upward spiral is simply an environment that encourages cooperation, understanding, and goodwill. That environment is created largely through the quality of our speech. Proverbs recommends six types of words that have the power to get a spiral headed in the right direction:

- **GENTLE WORDS**   - RIGHTEOUS WORDS
- SOOTHING WORDS   - **GRACIOUS WORDS**
- **TIMELY WORDS**   - PLEASANT WORDS

"The tongue of the wise makes knowledge acceptable," Proverbs says (15:2). A wise spouse learns how to express herself in a way that makes hard news easier to take; she knows how to make knowledge "acceptable." She does this not through the message itself but through the way the message is expressed.

FOUR
qualities of
caring words

1
Approval

2
Affection

3
Acceptance

4
Appreciation

Adapted from A Weekend
with the One You Love
by Art Hunt, 139

When you use gentle, gracious, and pleasant words with your mate, there's a much greater chance that you'll hear gentle, gracious, and pleasant words in return. Nobody likes a downward spiral; we all want to get along. To do so, someone has to have the discipline to choose soothing and righteous words and to turn that spiral skyward.

PASS THE DICE

Everybody knows that when you pass the dice, your turn is over. In conversation, things are seldom that clear. Anger grows when one partner turns a comment into a speech, a speech into a lecture, and a lecture into a filibuster. Everyone needs to know when his turn is over, and some have a better sense of timing than others.

Remember the order of play: "Listen long; talk short." In any conversation, listening should be the main course and speaking should be dessert. Say only what you need to say, then pass the dice. Put your focus on listening well; if your mate has not yet made himself clear, ask questions: "What did you mean by that? Can you explain a little more? Why do you feel that way?" When you make a habit of asking clarifying questions, your mate can afford to be brief.

But what about the case of a really heated argument? What do you do when no one's asking questions and no one wants to give up the dice?

In the days before cell phones, radio communicators had a handy technique for signaling the end of a message: They closed each transmission with the word, "Over," as in, "I'm calling you from Bob's house. Over." The helpful thing about this practice was that it let the listener know that the first person had finished speaking, that he could now respond, and that the silence he heard on the other end of the line was not the result of some equipment failure.

In conflict, it would be helpful if we had an equivalent for "Over." Sometimes your mate just seems to trail off. *. . . Is he finished? Is he thinking? Did he suddenly lose interest, or did he just run out of steam? If I say something, will he*

INSIGHT
Tact is the knack of making a point without making an enemy.
—*Howard W. Newton*

think I'm interrupting? If I say nothing, will he think I'm not paying attention? Earth to husband . . . Come in, husband. . . .

Some couples find that they have an easier time discussing heated issues on the telephone—or even in writing. That's because those modes of communication provide some helpful structure that interpersonal communication often lacks. To write a letter requires discipline, patience, and sequential thought. You have to collect your thoughts, select your words, and then present them in an orderly fashion. That would be a helpful approach to any conflict, but as we said before, we tend to treat the spoken word with casual disregard.

In the case of a heated disagreement, it can help to approach the discussion as if you were talking on the radio. Decide who will "broadcast" first; make your message brief, clear, and don't forget to "speak to heal." When you're finished, simply say, "I'm done," or "Your turn." To make things even simpler, pick an object that you can hold in your hand—a pencil, a coffee mug, even an actual pair of dice—and hand it to the person who speaks first. As long as he's holding that pencil, he's "got the floor." When he's finished, he surrenders the floor by handing you the object, sort of like a baton in a verbal relay race. It's just like passing the dice in a real board game. It may sound a little contrived, but that kind of visual reminder can make it very clear who should be speaking and who should be tuning in.

Just a reminder to turn to the appendix where you can create your own rules for fighting fair based on what you've found helpful in this chapter.

Mastering the ENDGAME

DOWNS

"If you spike that ball, I'm taking back my apology."

MASTERING THE ENDGAME

TEN reasons why relationship difficulties linger

1

Some people want to avoid the difficult feelings that could arise in a confrontation.

2

Some people take comfort in their difficulties. By complaining to others about the problem, they get sympathy.

3

Not resolving the difficulty is a way of punishing the other person.

4

Discord and disharmony may be preferable to no relationship at all.

5

Refusing to reconcile is a way to keep the relationship on one's own terms and remain in control.

(continued on page 75)

There was a classic movie made in the seventies called Love Story. *It's an intense and endearing story about the love between a young man and his young wife, who is dying of leukemia. At a climactic, tear-filled moment, the woman turns to her young husband and says, "Love means never having to say you're sorry."*

That's the point in the movie where we always double over in laughter and spill our Jujubees. If they had had the chance to be married a few months longer, they would have discovered what all married couples eventually catch on to. The sequel to the movie, had it ever been made, might have been entitled, *Love Story 2: Oops! Love Means Always Having to Say You're Sorry.*

Here in the world of real marriages, "I'm sorry" is a very necessary and often underused expression. So is the phrase "I forgive you." These two expressions form the "endgame" of conflict—the place where it all comes together or it all falls apart.

Not every difference of opinion requires an apology or forgiveness. But when you remember that conflict is not only about substance but style, there's usually *something* that needs to be made right at the end. Apology and forgiveness are the two most misunderstood rules of conflict. When we fail to master the endgame, our disagreements trail off but they never really *finish*; it's the endgame that brings a conflict to a satisfying close.

INSIGHT

Nobody ever forgets where he buried a hatchet.

—*Kin Hubbard*

HOW TO SAY YOU'RE SORRY

It sounds a little silly, doesn't it? What's so hard about saying, "I'm sorry"?

Apology is the place where your ego gets stretched across the altar. There is no way to utter the words, "I'm sorry"—and *mean* them—

without confronting your own pride. That's why we all like to use "pseudoapologies": clever, low-calorie, pride-preserving substitutes for the genuine article. Here are some classic examples of pseudo-apologies we've collected:

- **APOLOGY WITHOUT REMORSE:**
  "Logically, I'll admit you have a point."

- **PREMATURE APOLOGY:**
  "I'm sorry, I'm sorry; now can we drop the whole thing?"

- **APOLOGY OF EXPEDIENCE:**
  "All right, I'm sorry; now can we watch the game?"

- **ANGRY APOLOGY:**
  "OK! I'm sorry! Is *that* what you wanted?"

- **EXCUSING APOLOGY:**
  "I'm sorry; however . . ."

- **ABSENCE OF MALICE APOLOGY:**
  "I wasn't trying to hurt you."

- **PARTIAL APOLOGY:**
  "I'm sorry you feel bad."

- **NONRESPONSIBLE APOLOGY:**
  "I'm sorry this whole thing happened."

- **BITTER APOLOGY:**
  "I'm sorry for everything in the last ten years."

- **EVASIVE APOLOGY:**
  "Let's not be mad anymore."

- **CEASE-FIRE APOLOGY:**
  "I'm willing to call a truce if you are."

INSIGHT — **Excuses are always mixed with lies.** —*Arab proverb*

6
For some people, negative feelings are so familiar that they hold on to anger and shame just to feel alive.

7
Some people feel that they deserve to suffer and be unhappy.

8
Not reconciling allows some people to feel superior. The person wronged gets to feel righteous while the perpetrator is seen as the villain.

9
Some people are too proud to reconcile. Reconciling might require them to admit that they have also contributed to the difficulty.

10
Some people see no hope of reconciling.

—*Adapted from* Thank You for Being Such a Pain *by Mark Rosen, 149–50*

- **BURIAL APOLOGY:**

  "Let's just forget the whole thing."

- **PERSPECTIVE APOLOGY:**

  "We've got more important things to worry about than this."

- **BLAME-SHIFTING APOLOGY:**

  "I'm sorry you're so sensitive."

- **BLAME-SHARING APOLOGY:**

  "I guess we really blew it, didn't we?"

- **SELF-DEPRECATING APOLOGY:**

  "I don't know why you ever married me."

- **TRIVIALIZING APOLOGY:**

  "Hey, it's no big deal. Sorry."

There are endless varieties of pseudoapologies. Sometimes we seek to avoid true confession by giving a gift, doing a good deed, using distraction or humor, or even through having sex. What a testimony to human ingenuity! Many of these pseudo-apologies actually manage to use the words "I'm sorry" but never really apologize at all. When you use a pseudo-apology, you never have to admit guilt, take responsibility, or express remorse—and that's a handy technique. The pseudo-apologizer is often sorry—but never wrong. He never has to surrender his pride.

> **≡ Foul! ≡**
> Offering an apology may not make everything instantly right. Be careful not to show impatience: "I said I'm sorry; what do you want?"

What are the fundamentals of a good apology? Beverly Engel, in her book *The Power of Apology*, says that there are three essentials of any meaningful confession:

1 *Regret.* The desire to apologize needs to come from the realization that you have hurt someone or caused that person some difficulty.

2 **Responsibility.** For an apology to be effective, it must be clear that you are accepting total responsibility for your actions or inaction.

3 **Remedy.** Although you can't go back and undo or redo the past, you can do everything within your power to repair the harm you caused (67–68).

It's impossible to include these three elements in an apology without getting personally involved. *Regret* involves your emotions; it calls on you to feel bad about what you said or did, and it keeps you from offering impersonal, arm's-length admissions of guilt. *Responsibility* keeps you from blaming things on your circumstances, your upbringing, or your gene pool. It makes sure you personally own up to your actions or words. *Remedy* makes certain that your apology is more than just words. It offers to repair any damage you've done, and it promises to try not to repeat the offense again.

As you read these words, you might be saying to yourself, "Now hold on! That's a lot more than I'm willing to admit." That's the whole point; a good apology should feel a little bit awkward and a little too personal. After all, it's your ego that's about to take a hit—but that's OK. Our egos could use a little softening up from time to time, and there's no better way than through confession. As one writer put it, "True confession consists in telling our deed in such a way that our soul is changed in the telling of it."

What would a good apology sound like in practice? Try this one on for size: "I'm really sorry. I know I hurt your feelings and I feel terrible about it [regret]. You have every right to be angry with me. I shouldn't have said those things to you, and I have no excuse for talking to you like that [responsibility]. I'd like to discuss these things more often so I don't hold it all in and then blow up like that [remedy]."

The next time you go to offer an apology, make a three-point checklist in your mind. Make sure you include the three essential elements of regret, responsibility, and remedy; and you'll find you get a lot further

= **Foul!** =
This is the element of an apology that men often omit. But if your wife doesn't consider your words a sincere, heartfelt attempt to express sorrow, your apology won't be meaningful or convincing.

than you did with "Let's just forget the whole thing."

We're often asked, "Why should I accept 'total responsibility' when it's not all my fault? Why should *I* take all the blame?" There's an important clarification we need to make here. We're *not* encouraging you to apologize even when you don't think you're at fault. We *are* encouraging you to consider that there's plenty of room for error in a disagreement, and there may be *something* you should take responsibility for: your choice of words, your poor timing, your sarcastic attitude. . . . Standoffs occur when both partners stubbornly insist, "It's not my fault!" What they mean is "The major part of this disagreement is not my responsibility." Instead of focusing on what *isn't* our responsibility, we need to shift our focus to what *is*, and offer an apology for that. "Accepting total responsibility" does not mean that all the blame belongs to you; it means that, when it comes to the part that *is* yours, you need to be careful not to pass the buck to someone or something else.

Why are we putting so much emphasis on the correct way to apologize? Because of an ancient proverb that is a primary principle of the endgame: "A good apology is half forgiveness." When you do the work of apologizing well, when you're careful to include the elements of regret, responsibility, and remedy, you've done half of your partner's work for him. It's easy to forgive someone who has offered such a thorough and satisfying confession. It's far more difficult when you only offer a few contrite crumbs: "Sorry." When that happens, the work of forgiveness is all on your spouse's shoulders—if he feels like doing it at all.

DOING THE WORK OF FORGIVENESS

As hard as it is to offer a genuine apology, extending forgiveness to your husband or wife is even more of a challenge. Part of the difficulty is that we have higher expectations of our marriage partner than we do of anyone else. Every couple has a *history* of offense. In marriage we seldom get the chance to say, "I forgive you"; we always have to say, "I forgive you *again*."

Repeated offenses can create feelings of anger, despair, and hopelessness. When Peter asked Jesus, "Master, how many times do I forgive a brother or sister who hurts me? Seven?" Jesus replied,

"Seven! Hardly. Try seventy times seven" (Matthew 18:21–22 THE MESSAGE). That sounds awfully noble—but imagine what you would feel like after your husband's four-hundredth apology. Maybe that's why C. S. Lewis once wrote, "Everyone says forgiveness is a lovely idea, until they have something to forgive."

> **INSIGHT**
>
> **A happy marriage is the union of two good forgivers.**
>
> —*Robert Quillen*

We make the same mistake with the word *forgive* that we do with the word *love:* We think of both primarily as emotions, something that happens *to* us instead of something we play a part in. To be "in love" is to be overwhelmed by passion, longing, and desire. But what happens when stress, fatigue, or exhaustion causes the flames of love to dwindle temporarily? The answer is: You continue to *love*. Love is not just something you feel; it's something you *do*.

The same is true of forgiveness. To "forgive" does not simply mean "to have forgotten an offense; to feel that everything is back to normal again." If that's how you think of the word, you may be waiting a very long time to forgive. Forgiveness, like love, is something you do.

Ken Sande, in his book *The Peacemaker*, suggests that to say the words "I forgive you" is really to make four implicit promises. To forgive is to make a pledge to *do* four things:

1 *I promise I will not think about this incident,* because "Love does not dwell on conflict" (1 Corinthians 13:4).

2 *I promise I will not bring this incident up and use it against you,* because "Love . . . keeps no record of wrongs" (1 Corinthians 13:5).

3 *I promise I will not talk to others about this incident,* because "Love does not gossip" (1 Corinthians 13:6).

4 *I promise I will not allow this incident to stand between us or hinder our personal relationship,* because "Love breaks down walls" (1 Corinthians 13:4).

> **INSIGHT**
>
> One day Clara [Barton] was reminded of a vicious deed that someone had done to her years before. But she acted as if she had never heard of the incident! "Don't you remember it?" her friend asked. "No," came Clara's reply, "I distinctly remember forgetting it."
>
> —*From* Calm My Anxious Heart *by Linda Dillow, 73*

There is a great practical benefit in thinking of forgiveness this way. Instead of waiting around for forgiveness to happen *to* us, it gives us something to pursue. We can't prevent the occasional thought of a past offense from entering our minds, but we can refuse to dwell on it. We can resist the temptation to use past transgressions as tools of guilt or manipulation. And we can refuse to share intimate details with friends who may

Foul!
Never say behind your mate's back things that you would never say to his face.

violate our partner's trust. We can *do* things when we forgive. There's nothing like staying busy while we're waiting for the feelings of forgiveness to catch up.

What's the best way to say "I forgive you" to your mate? Just like apology, forgiveness has three essential elements: empathy, compassion, and grace.

Empathy. The word *empathy* literally means "to feel into." It means to recognize in someone else the same feelings, motivations, and drives that you feel yourself—both good *and* bad. As one writer said, "Forgiveness is the act of admitting we are like other people."

The Bible never allows us to think of ourselves as kings granting royal pardons, or as saints bestowing mercy on the unenlightened masses. When we look into the eyes of our erring mates, we should see *ourselves*. Empathy should lead us to say, "I've felt the same way, and I've done things just as bad."

The Word
Be gentle with one another, sensitive. Forgive one another as quickly and thoroughly as God in Christ forgave you.
—Ephesians 4:32 The Message

Compassion. Compassion is a deep longing to relieve suffering—your suffering, his suffering, and the suffering of your relationship. Compassion is love in action; it's the desire to repair the relationship, to make things right, and to get on with your lives. A compassionate response is one that eagerly extends forgiveness, rather than grudgingly granting a pardon.

Grace. Grace has three meanings that help us here: one is "generosity," and another is "a gift that is not deserved." A *gracious* expression of forgiveness is one that heaps on the mercy, freely and generously offering to let go of an offense. This is what James 1:5 means when it says, "If any of you lacks wisdom, let him ask of God, who gives to all generously and without reproach." God is a *gracious* giver, and we should seek to emulate Him. The third meaning of grace is "beauty, charm, or elegance." That means learning to extend forgiveness with style and class, in a way that doesn't grind your partner into the dust.

What would a good expression of forgiveness sound like? Here's a good model: "Thank you for saying, 'I'm sorry.' I know I'm not perfect either, and I know I've done things to hurt you in the past [empathy]. I forgive you! I'm really glad we talked about this. Let's not let this be a barrier between us—we've been getting along so well lately [compassion]! You are a wonderful husband/wife, and I love you very much [grace]."

If you paid close attention to our model apology earlier in this chapter, and if you match it with our example of forgiveness, you'll find that they fit together like a box and a lid. The apology is the box; into the box you place your disagreement, and forgiveness closes the lid. Apology and forgiveness work together to *enclose* a disagreement and to place it high up on a shelf, where it can be forgotten along with all the other remnants of the past.

The problem is when there *is* no box, or someone forgets the lid. Then conflicts can be messy things, always leaking out and requiring unexpected cleanup. What do you do when the box is never really closed?

WHEN IT'S ALL UP TO YOU

What do you do when you want to forgive but your mate refuses to apologize? If "a good apology is half forgiveness," what do you do when it's *all* up to you?

FIVE
things to do after a serious or long-lasting conflict

1. Apologize. Apologize sincerely and directly, and take 100 percent of the blame and responsibility. Now is not the time for a game of "who said what first."

2. Remind him that you admire and respect him. Let the person know that your actions were not meant as disrespectful, even though that is how they appeared.

3. Show your regret. Let the person know that you feel bad about your actions and promise him that they will not be repeated.

4. Demonstrate pain. He should know that you are in pain and suffering from both the guilt of your actions and the loss of the relationship.

5. Ask for forgiveness. Directly and specifically ask the person to forgive you.

—Adapted from Make Peace with Anyone *by David Lieberman, 103–4*

It's important here to make a distinction between *forgiveness* and *reconciliation*.

Remember the four promises of forgiveness? *I will not think about this incident, I will not bring this incident up and use it against you, I will not talk to others about this incident,* and *I will not allow this incident to stand between us.* Notice that they all begin with the word *I.* That means that forgiveness is a personal act, a one-sided commitment to extend empathy, compassion, and grace to your mate.

The Word
The north wind brings forth rain, and a backbiting tongue, an angry countenance.

PROVERBS 25:23

But reconciliation is the repair and restoration of the relationship, and that requires a team effort. *I* can forgive, but *we* have to reconcile. If you express this principle in mathematical terms, it looks something like this:

Apology + Forgiveness = ***Reconciliation***
Forgiveness + Nothing = ***Forgiveness***

When your partner extends an apology, a part of that apology is a suggested *remedy.* That means an apology is an invitation to work together to make repairs. When your partner continually refuses to apologize, reconciliation may become impossible. But even when there's no apology, it's still important to make a personal effort to forgive—because the alternative is too big a price to pay.

YOU OWE IT TO YOURSELF

Someone once said, "Carrying a grudge is like swallowing poison and waiting for the other person to die." When we refuse to forgive, it's like being taxed twice. First your mate offends you, and now *you* will pay the price for refusing to forgive.

Proverbs 11:17 says, "The merciful man does himself good, but the cruel man does himself harm." To withhold mercy is to harm

yourself; bitterness and resentment are like acids that can cor-
rode your entire outlook on life. You owe it to your mate to forgive
him, but you owe it to yourself too. Even when your mate refuses
to apologize, work through the mental steps of empathy, compas-
sion, and grace; and do what you can to keep the four promises of
forgiveness. In the process, your mate may soften and eventually
extend an apology. If not, you'll at least have done what you can to
relieve the burden from your own heart.

! **Just a reminder to turn to the appendix**
where you can create your own rules for fighting fair
based on what you've found helpful in this chapter.

$\equiv$ 11 $\equiv$

FOLLOW-Through

"I'm really sorry. Let's talk about how we can change you so I won't do that again."

FOLLOW-THROUGH

What's worse than a conflict just before bedtime? A conflict just before bedtime, and first thing in the morning, and just before bedtime . . . Some conflicts just won't seem to go away, and sometimes the reason is that we forget one crucial step—follow-through.

Some people think that the final words of any disagreement should be "I apologize" and "I forgive you." Not true. The final words of any conflict should be, "What do we need to change so that this doesn't happen again?" Follow-through means taking action, changing habits, and altering behavior until the source of the disagreement disappears—and that's why this step is so often overlooked.

Remember when Jesus healed the paralytic? He asked His listeners, "Which is easier, to say to the paralytic, 'Your sins are forgiven'; or to say, 'Arise, and take up your pallet and walk'?" (Mark 2:9). Answer: Actions are always harder than words. That's why actions speak so much louder—and that's why your words will sound hollow when follow-through is missing.

Which is easier, to say to your husband, "I'm sorry for leaving the car on empty again," or to stop for gas when it's raining? Which is easier, to say to your wife, "I'm sorry I called you 'irrational,'" or to remove a word from your vocabulary that you've been using for the last thirty-five years? Follow-through is often missing from conflict resolution because that's where you stop and pay the toll. Without follow-through, it's all just talk.

The biblical term for follow-through is *repentance,* which simply means "to turn around." Headed east? Try west. Going in harm's way? Don't go there. The next time you have a disagreement with your mate, end it with this question: "What would you like me to do differently so that this won't be a problem again?" And remember, it's all just talk unless you're willing to *act* on your mate's requests.

Do you have a disagreement that keeps coming back like a bad sausage? Then take a few minutes and ask yourself three questions:

What disagreement seems to recur for us regularly?

_____

_____

_____

_____

What attitudes, actions, or words are at the root of this conflict?

_____

_____

_____

_____

What could I do differently that would keep this issue from coming back again?

_____

_____

_____

_____

INSIGHT

What lies in our power to do, it lies in our power not to do.

—*Aristotle*

Just a reminder to turn to the appendix where you can create your own rules for fighting fair based on what you've found helpful in this chapter.

WHO Let the DOGS OUT?

"Reactor core meltdown! Reactor core meltdown! Why can't you just say 'I'm angry' like everybody else?"

WHO LET THE DOGS OUT?

FIVE
reasons women
get angry at
their husbands

1
Lack of caring

2
Lack of appreciation

3
Selfishness

4
Passivity or laziness

5
Poor listening habits

FIVE
reasons men
get angry at
their wives

1
Blame or faultfinding

2
Lack of respect

3
Dwelling on a point

4
Demanding

5
Controlling

et's face it. The real problem with conflict is anger.
You're having a peaceful, quiet conversation with your beloved spouse, when out of the blue he says something that strikes you the wrong way. He mentions that subject again, and he uses that word to do it. You feel your face flush and your ears begin to glow like twin curling irons. He knows not to go there. You've talked about it a thousand times, and yet there he is, like some mindless cow trampling the neighbor's daisies.

Before you can stop yourself, you actually call him a mindless cow. Now things really get lively.

Before you know it, you feel as if you're trapped in a car, careening down a winding hill, wondering why the brakes won't work. You've let the dogs out, and once the dogs are loose, it's hard to round them up again.

In a conflict, the problem is often not the disagreement itself but the way the disagreement is expressed. That's why we often say, "You only fight about an issue for the first three minutes; after that, you fight about the way you're fighting." Would you really object to a difference of opinion expressed in a kind, gracious, and loving manner? But thanks to anger, the style of our disagreements is often far from pleasant.

Why do we get so angry? The poet William Congreve once wrote, "Heaven hath no rage like love to hatred turned." That means that two lovers have the potential to get angrier with each other than any two perfect strangers. But why? Aren't we husband and wife? Aren't we life partners? Haven't we become *one flesh*?

Sybil Evans and Sherry Suib Cohen, in their book *Hot Buttons,* give four reasons why marital conflict can generate so much pain and anger:

INSIGHT

The Bible tells us to love our neighbors, and also to love our enemies; probably because they are generally the same people.

—G. K. Chesterton

1 ***Lovers have road maps to each other's hot buttons.*** When we feel rage and want to get even with someone, who knows better than a lover where her partner's hot button lies?

2 ***Neither is the boss.*** If you're the boss in your office, you can direct workers to do what you want.... But you can't direct your intimate partner to always do what you want, nor do you want him to be the boss....

3 ***You both have unreasonable expectations.*** Having a fight with a loved one hurts so much because expectations are so much higher—expectations you don't have about the outside world.

4 ***You wear masks.*** Ironically, the closer we are, the more we tend to mask a problem.

Because anger can have such devastating consequences, we come to think of it as inherently evil. But anger in and of itself is not wrong—in fact, it's a God-given emotion. If you read through the Bible, you will find that God Himself gets angry. In the perfect character of God, anger always serves one of two purposes: to protest what is evil or to protect what is good. Fallen human beings tend to get it backward; our anger often serves to protest what is good and protect what is evil. The problem is not anger itself but the way we use it.

Think of anger as the warning light on the dashboard of your soul. It's a passionate, persistent indicator that something is wrong that needs to be made right. What do you do when a warning light goes off in your car? You pull over and look under the hood. The warning light is telling you that something is wrong; it isn't telling you exactly what. It's your job to search for the cause and correct it.

INSIGHT
Anger is not only
inevitable, it is
necessary. Its
absence means
indifference, the
most disastrous
of all human
failings.
—*Arthur Ponsonby*

In the Bible, God often reminds angry people to stop and check under the hood. "Is it right for you to be angry about this?" God said to Jonah, who was grumbling about the fact that the Ninevites weren't going to be destroyed after all (see Jonah 4:4). Jonah, a prophet of God, found himself in the awkward position of protesting what is good (the abundant grace of God) and protecting what is evil (the destruction of an entire city). "Look under the hood," God was saying. "You'll find there's nothing wrong with what I'm doing, but there *is* something wrong with your heart."

INSIGHT
My life is in the
hands of any fool
who can make me
lose my temper.
—*Joseph Hunter*

"Why are you angry?" God said to Cain, who was homicidally jealous of his brother. "If you do what is right, will you not be accepted? But if you do not do what is right, sin is crouching at your door; it desires to have you, but you must master it" (Genesis 4:6–7 NIV). God visualized Cain's anger as a wild animal that would literally consume him if he didn't bring it under control. He did not, and history's first murder was the result.

Anger plays the same role in our own conflicts. We begin a disagreement with a desire to understand, cooperate, and compromise. But when anger starts to grow, our motives begin to subtly change. Instead of understanding, we add to the confusion; instead of cooperating, we stubbornly resist; instead of compromising, we demand our own way. Anger has caused us to lose sight of the objective of the game, and the wild animal is having a feast.

God's warning to Cain had two important reminders that are relevant to all of us: First, He reminded Cain of the destructive potential of anger, and second, He told him that it was *his* job to master it. So it is for us. Anger, left unchecked, can devour a relationship like a ravenous beast. It's our job to learn to tame the beast. We have five suggestions that can help.

INSIGHT — Anger is a bad counselor. —*French proverb*

CHECK THE ANGER LEVEL BEFORE, DURING, AND AFTER A CONFLICT

The objectives of the game of conflict are to understand each other better, to develop greater intimacy, and to clean up toxic waste. When it comes to anger, the crucial question to ask is: Is there too much anger between us to allow us to achieve our objectives? That question should be asked before, during, and after every conflict.

Before: In chapter 5 we described some attitudes that are necessary for conflict resolution to succeed, attitudes such as humility, responsibility, and a sense of humor. But as anger increases, those vital attitudes diminish. When a conflict is approaching and you sense storm clouds gathering above, stop and ask: Do we have cool enough heads to *resolve* this issue, or are we just going to end up shouting about it? When either or both of you feel too much anger to fight fair, then it's best to postpone—*not avoid*—the discussion.

> ## The Word
> A hot-tempered person starts fights; a cool-tempered person stops them.
> PROVERBS 15:18 NLT

During: As John Gottman says, "A harsh start-up simply dooms you to failure. So if you begin a discussion that way, you might as well pull the plug, take a breather, and start over" (Gottman, 27). There may come a point in a conflict when you're generating more heat than light, and that's when it's time to postpone. You can insist on pushing ahead, but if you do, you may learn a lesson from physics: Temperature increases with pressure. When the referee blows the whistle on anger, simply say to each other, "I think we're too angry to make any progress right now. Let's call a time-out and try again later."

After: Why is it important to check your anger level after the conflict is over? Because one of your objectives is to *clean up toxic waste*, and anger left over from one argument provides fodder for the next. Remember, there are three conversations taking place within your discussion: facts, feelings, and identity. Sometimes we make the mistake of addressing the facts but ignoring hurt feelings, and then the conflict

SEVEN effects of adrenaline on the body

1 Blood pressure increases.

2 Breathing speeds up.

3 Extra sugar is released into the blood.

4 The pupils dilate.

5 Blood is diverted to the brain and muscles.

6 Muscle tension increases.

7 Perspiration increases.

***TIP*—IF ANGER CAUSES YOU TO POSTPONE A CONFLICT, RESCHEDULE YOUR DISCUSSION FOR A SPECIFIC TIME AND PLACE. KNOWING THAT YOU WILL TALK IT OVER KEEPS THE ANGER FROM GROWING.

SIX
things that
create an
environment
for anger

1. STRESS
We're pulled in every direction, busy and going nowhere fast, having to do more with less time.

2. EVIL
Satan is the great confuser and the ultimate liar. He magnifies our weaknesses and fears and uses them as wedges that come between us.

3. FALSE EXPECTATIONS
It takes a lot of humility, grace, and constant work at understanding what is reasonable for you and your spouse to expect from each other.

4. SELFISHNESS
Selfishness, so rampant in our culture, creates an "island of me," when we should be sharing the "island of we."

5. SCRIPTS FROM THE PAST
A lot of our behavior is influenced by scripts that were written for us long ago.

6. SPEED
Intimacy takes time, but when we live life in the fast lane, intimacy falls by the wayside.

Adapted from Tim and Julie Clinton in sidebar entitled, "How 'Disaffection' Starts," Moody magazine, Nov/Dec 2002, 25

isn't really resolved. Make it a practice to finish a disagreement by asking, "Did we cover everything? How do you feel right now?"

DON'T TRANSLATE HURT INTO ANGER

There is an entire range of negative human emotions: hurt, fear, anxiety, despair, and more. But in our society, there is only one negative emotion that is viewed as truly "masculine," and that's anger. For that reason, men grow up learning to be master translators of negative emotions. Men feel fearful, so they get angry. They feel insecure, so they get angry. They get their feelings hurt, so they get angry. No wonder we have a nation of angry men.

The problem is, all of the other negative emotions arouse feelings of sympathy and compassion in our partners—all except anger. Are you worried? Come here and let's talk about it. Are you afraid? Let me give you a hug. Are you angry? Well, why are you taking it out on me? Drawing near to an angry person is like cuddling up with a porcupine. Sadly, anger often pushes your partner away at the very time you need her most. It's hard not to take your mate's anger personally; learning to see past the anger is an art, and it requires wisdom and patience.

When we sense anger beginning to grow, we need to stop and ask ourselves God's timeless diagnostic question: "Why are you angry?" It's important to learn to identify our true emotions. Try to look at the root of your feelings: What are you really feeling, and why? Try to understand whether it's really anger you're dealing with, or whether your anger is just a façade for something you're really feeling underneath.

MAKE IT YOUR GOAL TO HAVE
PROPORTIONATE CONFLICTS

A wise approach to conflict is to have big fights about big things, and little fights about little things. This is what we call "proportionate conflict." The wisdom behind this approach is that, after several years of marriage, there are very few "big things" left to discuss, and you can then settle down to a lifetime of occasional minor differences of opinion.

What's really exhausting is when you find yourself constantly having major squabbles over relatively minor issues. When that happens, it's an indicator that one of you is *borrowing* anger. When you experience anger but fail to resolve it, it doesn't just go away; it seeps down into an underground reservoir beneath your house. Over time, as it collects, it builds pressure; when a conflict comes along, it taps into that underground reservoir and the pent-up pressure is released. When a minor disagreement erupts with geyserlike force, it's time to check the level of the underground reservoir. Ask your partner, "Why are you *so* angry? Is anything else contributing to your anger? Are you angry at anyone else besides me?"

INSIGHT

If a small thing has the power to make you angry, does that not indicate something about your size?

—*Sydney J. Harris*

FOUR conditions commonly mistaken for anger

1
Fatigue

2
Embarrassment

3
Frustration

4
Rejection

—*Adapted from* Emotions: Can You Trust Them? *by James Dobson, 88–89*

DON'T LET ANGER GO BAD

The book of Ephesians gives a surprising piece of advice: "Be angry, and yet do not sin" (4:26). Shouldn't it read, "Do not sin by being angry"? Apparently anger and sin are not the same thing; it must be possible to be angry without stepping over the line.

What is it that tends to make anger go bad? Ephesians goes on to say, "Do not let the sun go down on your anger, and do not give the devil an opportunity" (vv. 26–27). Anger is a natural product; it's made without additives or preservatives, and it has a shelf life just like the cottage cheese in your refrigerator. What is the shelf life of anger? According to Ephesians, anger is best "consumed" the same day it originates. Anger was never intended to be stored, and when you leave it on the shelf too long, it can become host to a variety of repugnant, foul-smelling parasites.

Ephesians warns us that smoldering anger gives the devil a "foothold" (NIV). A foothold provides the same advantage for the devil that

---

TIP—TO HELP PUT AN ISSUE IN PERSPECTIVE, WHEN A DISAGREEMENT BEGINS, ASK YOUR MATE, "ON A SCALE FROM ONE TO TEN, HOW IMPORTANT IS THIS TO YOU?"

TEN
results of mishandled anger according to Proverbs

1
It alienates loved ones.

2
It causes reckless action.

3
It leads to foolish things.

4
It causes mistakes.

5
It creates quarrels.

6
It causes loss of control.

7
It ensnares.

8
It takes away peace.

9
It stirs up trouble.

10
It causes strife.

it does for a rock climber; it provides a solid footing from which the Enemy can push off into even deeper areas of our lives.

Cleaning out the fridge is a periodic necessity; we need to do the equivalent in our relationships by searching for festering pockets of anger hidden on the bottom shelf. Ask your mate from time to time, "Are we OK? Is there anything we need to clear up?" Do your best to keep short accounts, and don't give anger the chance to spoil.

DEAL WITH ANGER ONE STEP AT A TIME

In his book *How to Really Love Your Teenager,* psychiatrist Ross Campbell encourages us to think of our style of expressing anger as a *process*—a process that has to be improved one step at a time. In Campbell's view, it does little good to say to yourself, *I need to stop getting angry.* Remember, anger is a God-given emotion, and it isn't going to simply go away, any more than joy or sadness will. As we said earlier, when you feel anger coming on, it's always wise to stop and ask, "Why am I angry? Is it right for me to be angry about this?" But once you've considered this, the goal is to consider how you currently *express* your anger, and to work to improve one step at a time. Campbell calls this approach the "Anger Ladder."

> ### The Word
> Keep a sharp eye out for weeds of bitter discontent. A thistle or two gone to seed can ruin a whole garden in no time.
> HEBREWS 12:15 THE MESSAGE

Think of your style of expressing anger as a ladder with a series of rungs. Where are you standing on the Anger Ladder right now? What would be the next rung up the ladder for you? Think about one change you could make that would improve the manner or intensity of your expression of anger.

Suppose your current style of expressing anger is to shout at your mate. If that's the case, then make a commitment not to shout anymore. Just like that? Yes, that small a change is within your power to make with just a little self-control. You still might say some unpleasant things from time to time, but if you stop shouting, you've at least climbed one rung up the Anger Ladder, and that's progress—just ask your mate. And ask your mate to be patient with you as you climb the Anger Ladder. Some habits are more ingrained than others. But let her know that, though you may fail from time to time, you'll do your best to keep moving upward.

Does one rung sound like too small a step? Some people think so. They express their anger inappropriately and then promise their mate that they will climb the entire Anger Ladder in a single day. But ladders are best climbed one rung at a time. Campbell reminds us that anger responses are learned behaviors; they took time to form, and they can take time to change. One rung may sound like a small step, but it is a step forward. Remember, one step up the Anger Ladder might have saved Abel's life.

If you're not sure where you are on the Anger Ladder, ask your mate—and while you're at it, ask her where she'd like you to be. When it comes to expressing anger, you'll find that any improvement will be welcomed.

! **Just a reminder to turn to the appendix where you can create your own rules for fighting fair based on what you've found helpful in this chapter.**

= 13 =

Putting It **All** Together

*"You say nothing is bothering you,
but your body language is hinting at something else."*

PUTTING IT ALL TOGETHER

Something is bothering you. It's something he said or something he did—for the third time this week. Or maybe it's something that happened last week that you haven't had a chance to bring up, but it's been the burr in your burrito ever since. There's no doubt about it; you're going to have a disagreement—so what do you do first? How do you start this thing, and where do you go from there?

Of course, asking how to start a conflict is like asking how to start childbirth—it has a way of happening on its own. But when you let a conflict run its own course, there's no telling where it will go—and sometimes there's no stopping it either. How do you conduct a conflict so that it leads to a peaceful and constructive conclusion?

Here's a six-step process that brings together everything we've discussed so far. First, remember a couple of important preliminary steps. . . .

TIP—IT'S IMPORTANT TO REMEMBER WHO WE ARE IN CHRIST AND THAT HE LOVES US. THAT SHOULD HELP US HEAR OUR SHORTCOMINGS FROM OTHERS MORE GRACIOUSLY.

WARM UP AND STRETCH OUT (CHAPTERS 7 AND 12)

The warm-up is the most commonly overlooked part of any game—and the most common source of injury and regret later on. Before approaching your mate, check in with your Creator. Allow God to remind you of your own forgiveness from Him, and ask Him for the same spirit of grace, wisdom, and gentleness when you talk with your partner. Remember, forgiven people are forgiving people.

And don't forget to check that anger level! Remember the objectives of the upcoming game: to gain understanding, to increase intimacy, and to clean up toxic waste. If you're too angry to focus on those objectives, this is not the time to argue.

These two steps are extremely important! Because they're only mental processes, some people think they contribute nothing to the actual game—just as some people think that stretching has nothing to do with the actual race; then they pull up lame later. This simple warm-up will put you in the right frame of mind before you ever open your mouth.

SCHEDULE THE GAME (CHAPTER 6)

Despite the helpful guidelines we described in chapter 6, requesting a "discussion" can still be like asking if your spouse wants a root canal. Two additional tips can help you to schedule a game with a willing partner.

First, *request a meeting; don't demand one.* John Churton Collins once advised, "Never claim as a right what you can ask as a favor." Though it sometimes irritates our pride, there is great persuasive power in the simple words, "May I ask a favor?"

Second, *speak for yourself.* Let the focus of your first words be your desire, not his behavior. Try saying, "There's something I'd like to talk over," or "There's something on my mind," instead of, "We have to talk," or "You did it again." By the way, it helps to request a dialogue and not a lecture. Try saying, "I'd like to talk *with* you," and not, "I need to talk *to* you."

> **INSIGHT**
> From a good beginning comes a good end.
> —*John Heywood*

TIP—TELLING YOUR MATE YOU WANT TO TALK ARE THE FIRST WORDS OF YOUR DISAGREEMENT. BE ESPECIALLY CAREFUL OF YOUR TONE OF VOICE AND ATTITUDE!

PLAY THE GAME

With your warm-up completed and your scheduled meeting at hand, what's the next step? Here's the six-step process:

1 *Step 1: Get all the help you can get (chapter 7).* Remember, conflict is essentially a spiritual activity. That's why we recommend that you take a few minutes to pray together before the conversation gets under way. Pray for seeing eyes and hearing ears—remember they're gifts of the Lord (Proverbs 20:12). Ask for grace to give to each other, and pray that God would act as your referee—then pull up a chair to remind both of you of His presence.

2 *Step 2: Plan your opening remarks.* Remember John Gottman's caution: "The research shows that if your discussion begins with a harsh start-up, it will inevitably end on a negative note, even if there are a lot of attempts to 'make nice' in between." Opening remarks are the most important words we'll say, yet sometimes we approach a disagreement with little thought about what those first words will be or how they should be spoken. Considering the relative importance of opening remarks, why not increase your chances of a warm reception by framing your remarks in one of these ways?

- *Introduce a complaint with a praise:* "You are such a great husband/wife/mom/dad. . . ."

- *Express approval before disapproval:* "I don't know what we would do without you around here. . . ."

- *Point out what was done right before you mention what was done wrong:* "I want to thank you for going out of your way to . . ."

- *Find fault without assigning blame:* "I'm not blaming you, but I'm concerned about something. . . ."

- *Recognize good intentions before pointing out bad actions:* "I know you meant well, and I appreciate what you were trying to do, but . . ."

If these approaches seem overly cautious to you, remember the disproportionate power of your opening remarks. This is your chance to begin on a positive note, to display a gracious and generous attitude, and to introduce a topic without making your mate the bad guy. That's no small feat! Psalm 100:4 tells us, "Enter His gates with thanksgiving and His courts

INSIGHT

There is a great difference between knowing a thing and understanding it.

—*Charles Kettering*

with praise." No human being should barge into the presence of God without first preparing his heart and adjusting his perspective. Those corrections are made through expressions of thanksgiving and praise; you'll find they have a similar effect when you charge into conflict with your mate.

One important reminder: *The preceding suggestions are not formulas.* Don't simply throw out the words, "You're a nice guy, BUT . . ." If you do, your mate will ignore those first few crumbs and wait for the other shoe to drop. Your introductory words should be genuine, heartfelt, thorough expressions of praise, approval, or gratitude. If you treat our suggestions as mechanical procedures, your mate will quickly recognize it, and your words will have the opposite effect you were hoping for—they will serve to accelerate your conflict, because your mate will feel manipulated or demeaned.

3 *Step 3: State your case.* This is the "meat" of the disagreement, the part that we often cut to too quickly—with unpleasant results. What's the best way to voice a criticism, complaint, or objection? Try this simple, four-point outline to keep you on track and out of trouble:

Relate what she did or said. The goal here is to focus on her behavior and resist the temptation to draw conclusions about her character or motives. You need to say, "Yesterday, you said . . ." and not, "Yesterday, you were just being obnoxious."

Explain any consequences of her words or actions. What happened because of what she did? Were the kids frightened? Did you lose money? Did she lose respect or damage her reputation? Explain the consequences of her actions, and it will give your words their proper priority.

Describe how it made you feel. One of the consequences of her actions was the effect they had on you. Did you feel ignored, humiliated, disrespected, or shamed? Don't make this complaint just a logical objection; describe how it affected your relationship with her.

Tell her what you want her to do. Strangely, this step is often skipped.

FIVE principles of loving confrontation

1
Confront caringly.
Confront primarily to express real concern for another.

2
Confront gently.
Do not draw out more than you have put into the relationship.

3
Confront constructively.
Take into consideration any possible interpretations of blaming, shaming, punishing.

4
Confront acceptingly.
Little is to be gained by impugning motives or evaluating another's hopes, wishes, goals.

5
Confront clearly.
Do not state an interpretation as though it were a fact.

—Adapted from Caring Enough to Confront *by David Augsburger, 58–59*

FOUR
thoughts
to do your
best to resist

1
By now he should
know what to do.

2
I shouldn't have to tell
her what to do.

3
I told him what to
do before, and he
didn't do it.

4
If he cared, he would do
it without being told.

If you happen to be an indirect or nonassertive communicator, those first three points seem to be all that's necessary. I told you what you did, what happened next, and how it made me feel; the rest is up to you. If you care, you'll know what to do.

And she does know what to do. She'll do what *she* thinks she should do—but probably not what you want her to do. She won't know what you want unless you tell her. To some of us, it just feels too demanding to come right out and say, "I want you to . . ." But that's the only way to bring the subject to a conclusion. If you skip this step, you may find yourself having the same discussion again.

4 *Step 4: Express apology and forgiveness (chapter 10).* As we said before, when we fail to apologize and forgive, our disagreements trail off, but they never really *finish*. It's the endgame that brings a conflict to a satisfying close.

Is there something you need to apologize for? Think not only about the substance of the disagreement but the style: Were you disrespectful, condescending, or just plain mean? Did you express your anger inappropriately? Do you need to say "I'm sorry" for the attitude behind your words?

Remember, an apology without forgiveness is like a box with no lid. Do you need to offer forgiveness? Can you extend empathy, compassion, and grace to your mate? And if he isn't offering an apology, can you at least do your best not to let bitterness take root?

Express apology and forgiveness sincerely, generously, and completely. Close the lid firmly on the box, hammer in a few nails, and put the disagreement behind you.

5 *Step 5: Remind him of your love and commitment (chapter 16).* James Dobson recommends that after disciplining a child, "he should be welcomed with open, warm, loving arms. At that moment you can talk heart to heart. You can tell him how much you love him, and how important he is to you" (*Dare to Discipline*, 23). That advice isn't just important with kids. Every conflict should begin and end with an expression of love and commitment; that sets the entire disagreement in an environment of acceptance, rather than disapproval or rejection.

When the conflict comes to a close, offer your partner a reassuring hug. You'll find that it serves as a litmus test; the warmth of the response will tell you whether the discussion is really over or not. Even after a sincere apology and forgiveness, it may still take a little time for the hurts to heal and the climate to be restored.

6 *Step 6: Follow-through (chapter 11).* Here's the second-most overlooked step in a conflict—and when it is overlooked, it's sure to be the start of the next one. We've said a partner should tell her spouse what she wants him to do differently; when she tells you, you need to do your best to do it. You listened, you understand, and you feel bad— but what are you going to *do*?

The best way to prevent the next conflict from happening is by changing the circumstances that made this one occur. You're always late? Set the clock ahead fifteen minutes. Lost the receipts again? Buy an accordion file. Granted, it isn't always that easy, but even making the effort will show your mate that you're taking her wishes seriously.

WHAT ABOUT UNSCHEDULED GAMES?

We know what you're thinking: *Most of our conflicts aren't planned events. They come out of nowhere and catch us off guard. We make most of our mistakes because we never have a chance to "plan our opening remarks." Sometimes we're in the middle of a conflict before one of us even knows it's under way!* What do you do when there just isn't time to follow a six-step process? What about those *unscheduled* games?

When you find yourself in the middle of an unexpected disagreement, we recommend an abbreviated four-step process to undo the damage and get back on track:

Hit the brakes and back up.

The biggest problem with unexpected conflicts is the damage you do before you even know you've begun. When you steer your car down

INSIGHT
Great is the art of beginning, but greater the art is of ending.
—*Henry Wadsworth Longfellow*

INSIGHT
Remaining silent, building up resentments, and distancing yourself from others instead of letting them know how they have hurt you can cause as many problems in interpersonal relationships as not apologizing when you have hurt someone.
—*From* The Power of Apology *by Beverly Engel,* 121

that one-way street, the first thing you do is stop and back up. You might actually say, "Hold it. I'm not sure how this started, but I think we're both saying things we don't mean. I'm sorry. Can we back up and try again?"

Reword your opening remarks.

Now that you've brought the car to a stop, push gently on the gas. You've told her what you *didn't* mean to say—now try again. Remember our principles for opening remarks; say all the nice things you would have said if you'd only had a little more time to plan ahead.

State your case—if you can.

In an unexpected conflict, you need to check the anger level all along the way. Has a harsh start-up left you with nowhere to go? Is there too much anger to allow you to talk calmly and productively? Are there too many hurt feelings to proceed? Then apologize for the harsh start-up and postpone the discussion to a later time.

If stopping, backing up, and rewording your opening remarks did the trick, then try the issue again. But proceed with caution; you're driving on broken glass.

Apologize, forgive, and communicate love.

Even a brief exchange is still a conflict, and it needs to be concluded. A little unresolved disagreement is like a paper cut; it can cause a surprising amount of annoyance for such a tiny wound. Cauterize the wound: Say you're sorry, offer forgiveness, and don't forget that hug and kiss.

If you follow the simple order of events we've outlined above, will it guarantee that your disagreements will all come to a peaceful and productive end? Unfortunately, no. Our procedures are not mathematical formulas, and your mate is a human being who is just as impulsive, unpredictable, and bewildering as . . . *you* are.

A conflict can be as confusing as the proverbial Gordian knot, and it isn't always easy to unravel. But a conflict becomes even more perplexing when there are no goals, no structure, no rules, and no referee. We offer these guidelines not to guarantee success but to help pave a clear and ordered path to the goal—to help you win at conflict without losing at love.

! **Just a reminder to turn to the appendix where you can create your own rules for fighting fair based on what you've found helpful in this chapter.**

14

Penalties and FOULS

"Perhaps that last word was a tad strong."

PENALTIES AND FOULS

Every board game has its own penalties and fouls. With every roll of the dice, there is the chance that you will land on one of those accursed spaces marked "GO BACK THREE SPACES." The whole point of the game is to be the first to advance your token to Boardwalk or Millionaire Acres or Candy Land, depending on the age of your kids. There's nothing worse than watching your playing piece make the agonizing slide down that long, red chute, realizing that you'll have to spend the next ten minutes revisiting ground that you already covered. It's even worse when you land on the space marked "MISS ONE TURN." Now you have the particular thrill of watching everyone else advance their pieces while you sit back and try to look interested.

As we said before, every game has a goal, and no one wants to waste her time sitting on the sidelines or recovering lost ground. But every game has its penalties and fouls that will cause you to do just that, and conflict is no exception. Here, in no particular order, is a list of penalties and fouls guaranteed to cause you to stall or lose ground in any disagreement.

BLAME: "THIS IS ALL YOUR FAULT."

If you want to shift an argument into neutral, spend your time trying to identify the real culprit in your disagreement. Whose fault is it? Who owns this problem, and who is the innocent bystander? The problem is that in most cases, neither of you feels entirely responsible for the conflict. No matter what you said or did, your partner always seems to share *some* part of the blame.

Don't forget what we said in chapter 2. Every argument has three invisible conversations that take place within it: the "What happened?" conversation, the "Feelings" conversation, and the "Identity" conversation. That means that while you're blaming your mate for "what happened," he may be blaming you for hurting his "feelings." In an argument there are different things to be responsible *for,* and it rarely helps to try to pin the blame on one party alone. It's helpful to make a simple mental adjustment: Try to think of your relationship as a third party, almost like another person. There's me, there's you, and there's *us.* Whenever there's a problem in the relationship, regardless of who appears at first to be at fault, *we* have a problem. That little shift in attitude will encourage you to search for your own part in the problem, and it will keep you from steering the conflict up a dead-end street.

But aren't there times when one person *is* to blame? Is it wrong to ask your partner to accept responsibility for his actions? Not at all; the question is, what's the best way to get your partner to accept responsibility? You'll find it much more productive to simply discuss the issue until your individual contributions to the problem become clear. It's easier on the ego to choose to accept responsibility than to have it dumped in your lap.

THE QUESTION OF ORIGINS: "YOU STARTED THIS."

Similar to the foul of blaming and faultfinding is the tendency to try to identify the originator of the disagreement. If you started it, after all, then the problem really belongs to you. "I was just standing here, minding my own business, when you said . . ." But of course, couples rarely agree on precisely when a disagreement began. Each believes that his or her own anger is nothing more than a response to something the partner did first. And the fact is, they're both right: For him, the argument began five minutes ago when she said, "___." For her, the argument began last Tuesday when he ___. For

---

INSIGHT
Quarrels would not last long if the fault were on one side only.

—François de la Rochefoucauld

TIP—BECAUSE MEN PLACE SO MUCH EMPHASIS ON PERFORMANCE AND COMPETENCE, THEY ARE ESPECIALLY SENSITIVE TO BLAME.

The Word
God sets himself against the proud, but he shows favor to the humble.
1 PETER 5:5 NLT

each of them, their anger or frustration is just a response—but they're responding to different things.

For this reason, it's usually a waste of time to try to agree on what started all this. You may find it helpful to discuss what started it for *you,* but only to help your partner better understand your perspective. Every argument has two different starting points; the goal is to have the same finish line.

HISTORY LESSONS: "THIS IS LIKE THE TIME WHEN YOU . . ."

It's human nature to search for patterns in complex situations; patterns help us make sense of the strange and unfamiliar. But it doesn't help a conflict when we insist on comparing the present situation to something from the past. We hope that it might be a kind of shortcut to refer to the historical record. Why go into all the confusing intricacies of this disagreement when we can just compare it to one from the past? "Remember the fight we had about ___? This is just like that one. You were wrong then, and you're wrong now."

But your mate isn't likely to agree. It feels as if you're trying to establish some kind of recurring pattern. "You see? You're doing that thing again." To her, this disagreement is a unique situation; it may have *some* similarities to the past, but your attempt to equate this disagreement with one from days of yore feels to her like an evasion. Never mind about *then;* what about *now?* Are you willing to deal with the messiness of *this* situation, or are you going to simply pigeonhole it in the past?

History lessons are almost always unproductive, because they take the discussion on a tangent. Instead of talking about the present, now we're arguing about the past too. Is this like that other time? Is it *just* like that other time? It's difficult enough to resolve the problems of the present day; having to deal with all of history can be downright exhausting.

READING FROM THE RECORD: "YOUR EXACT WORDS WERE . . ."

Sometimes a conflict accelerates over the use of a specific word or phrase. In those situations, you want your partner to face up to the source of the offense. "That's not what you said. What you said was ___." But much to your dismay, your partner often disagrees about what was actually said, leading you once again on a tangent: Who said what to whom?

We've all seen enough TV courtroom dramas to know that, when there is confusion over a piece of testimony, all we have to do is send for the court reporter to read from the official record. We hope that we'll be able to do the same thing in our own conflicts, substituting our own fallible memory for the written transcript. It doesn't work.

Human communication is a multichannel event. It involves subtle facial expressions, minute variations in tone of voice, and almost imperceptible movements of the eyes. And words themselves are not simple; they have connotations and nuances that sometimes communicate far more than the word itself. When an offensive word or phrase is spoken, the offense is often the collective impact of a multichannel message. What was it that really bothered you—the word itself, the connotation of the word, or the way that it was spoken? All are a part of what was *said*.

And that's why we can't always agree on the official record. So why bother? Instead of insisting on your version of what was said, ask him to say it in a different way. Keep the focus on the meaning and not on the words themselves. Try to listen for the hurt, fear, or disappointment in what your mate is really trying to communicate. Be compassionate as you listen.

DEFENSIVENESS: "IT WASN'T MY FAULT."

In chapter 8 we asked the question, "What does conflict mean to you?" For some of us, conflict instinctively suggests accusation, criticism, and condemnation. The beginning of any disagreement feels like a personal attack, and so our first impulse is to raise the shields

---

SEVEN ways to handle criticism constructively

1
Listen.

2
Avoid retaliation.

3
Don't respond immediately.

4
Respect the criticism.

5
Be honest with yourself.

6
Forgive.

7
Have a good attitude.

—*Kyle Liedtke*

INSIGHT

Memory is a complicated thing, a relative to truth, but not its twin.

—*Barbara Kingsolver*

INSIGHT

Nothing so needs reforming as other people's habits.

—*Mark Twain*

and arm the photon torpedoes. But we can be so busy trying to defend ourselves that we never understand the true nature of the attack—or whether it's really an attack at all.

For some people, listening is what they pretend to do while they're thinking of what they want to say next. This is especially true of the defensive person, whose focus is less on the message being sent than on the impregnable fortress he's building in response. All he ever seems to say is, "That's not true. . . . There's a reason for that. . . . I never . . . I didn't . . ." When the fortress is impenetrable, no messages can get in *or* out. There can be no understanding, and without understanding there can be no forward movement in a conflict. That's too great a price to pay for security.

Here's an important tip: Helping a mate overcome his defensiveness will require effort by both of you. Yes, he may be too sensitive, but you may be unaware of words, gestures, or tones of voice that automatically raise his defensive barriers. When your mate raises his shield, it's wise to ask yourself, "Have I drawn my sword?"

The Word

Don't repay evil for evil. Don't retaliate when people say unkind things about you. Instead, pay them back with a blessing. That is what God wants you to do, and he will bless you for it.

—1 PETER 3:9 NLT

REVERSAL: "ME? WHAT ABOUT WHEN YOU . . . ?"

Reversal is a form of defensiveness. Sometimes our objection is not to a specific word or phrase but to the person raising the objection. "How can *you* accuse *me*? Why do you criticize me for this when I overlook so many things with you? What about all the times when you . . . ?"

While *defensiveness* is a process of building a protective barrier, *reversal* is the strategy of achieving victory through quick counterattack. Reversal is like seeing a live grenade roll into my bunker. Instead of diving for cover, I grab the grenade and lob it back before it has time to explode. Instead of carefully considering your words, I simply throw them back at you. After all, if they can hurt me, they can hurt you too.

Another form of reversal is to respond to a complaint with an unrelated complaint of your own. Instead of throwing your spouse's own words back at her ("So I'm lazy? Well, so are you!"), this approach simply ignores the attack and mounts an attack of its own. "So I'm lazy? Well, I'd rather be lazy than sloppy!" The goal is to shift your partner's focus from furthering *her* complaint to defending herself from one of your own.

The problem, as with all defensive responses, is that you're so busy returning fire that you never take time to consider the nature of the attack. Why did she throw the grenade in the first place? Is it possible that she had a good reason? And if you throw this one back, is she just going to lob another? As painful as it may sound, we have to let the grenades go off. We have to be disciplined and courageous enough to patiently consider our mate's complaint, and try to save our own for another time.

COMPARISON: "WHY CAN'T YOU BE LIKE MIKE?"

One of the most painful components of any conflict is the feeling of disapproval that seems to go with it. If you're already feeling a lack of praise, encouragement, and grace—things we'll talk about in chapter 16—then a conflict is even more likely to feel like a personal failure. It's hard enough to feel that you're doing badly; it's even worse to be reminded that someone else is doing better.

We sometimes use comparisons simply to help clarify our meaning. "I want you to spend more time with me the way Mike does with his wife." But to a person sensing disapproval, it sounds more like, "Why are you a failure? Why can't you be a success like Mike?" That wasn't the *intended* message, but comparisons attract unintended meanings like moths to a flame.

Is your complaint that your husband doesn't spend enough time with you or that your husband isn't Mike? The desire to clarify is a good one, but avoid the temptation to illustrate through comparison to others. Comparisons have a way of generating conflicts of their own.

THREE common forms of reversal

1
Historical:
"What about last summer when you . . . ?"

2
Comparison:
"This isn't half as bad as when you . . ."

3
Irrelevant:
"Well, I'd rather be lazy than sloppy."

TIP—YOU CAN ARGUE ABOUT A HUNDRED TOPICS AT ONCE, BUT YOU CAN ONLY RESOLVE ONE AT A TIME.

FOUR
tangents that
come from
making
comparisons

1

"You seem to pay a lot
of attention to Mike."

2

"Apparently you wish
you were married to
Mike."

3

"Let me tell you all
the ways that Mike
is a failure."

4

"I'm a lot better
than Mike at . . ."

INSIGHT

Logic: another
term for "thinking
like I do."

BUTTON-PUSHING: "WHY DO YOU HAVE TO ACT SO CHILDISHLY?"

Buttons are control devices; they serve as switches that activate other devices. A button is always wired to something, and it isn't always obvious what. Sometimes a very large and dangerous machine can be set in motion at the touch of a very small button.

All of us have "buttons": certain words, expressions, attitudes, or gestures that set us off—sometimes, we're not even sure why. No one knows your buttons better than your mate. Marriage grants your partner access to your Master Control Panel, a tempting array of buttons of all colors and sizes. Over the course of marriage, we systematically push each one to find out what it does. Most seem to have little effect, but some actually launch ballistic missiles. We always remember where those buttons are.

When you tire of a disagreement, or when it isn't going your way, it's always tempting to push one of those buttons and initiate a nuclear catastrophe. But make no mistake; that's exactly what will happen. No one leans on the big red button by accident; your mate knows it and so do you. By pushing your mate's button, you will completely obscure the original conflict, and you'll be left with yet another conflict to resolve at a later time.

ANALOGIES: "THIS PROBLEM IS LIKE AN OAK TREE. . . ."

To you, this problem *is* like an oak tree—but to your mate it's not. That's the problem with analogies; at some points the comparison is accurate, but at other points it isn't true at all. When you say, "Our love is like a red, red rose," do you mean that our love is rare and beautiful or that it seems to wither and die every winter?

Some of us are more visual thinkers than others. For those who are, it's always a temptation to clarify through illustration. But be careful: Though similes and metaphors can be helpful tools for under-

INSIGHT

Selfishness is not
living as one wishes
to live; it is asking
others to live as one
wishes to live.

—*Oscar Wilde*

standing, they can also lead to tangents. Suddenly, instead of talking about the original issue, we find ourselves arguing about whether our problem is really like an oak tree or not, or whether it's more like a ponderosa pine. Using an analogy is like offering a handshake; if your partner accepts it, fine. If not, forget it and get on with the conversation.

LOGIC: "WHY CAN'T YOU BE MORE RATIONAL?"

There are all kinds of paths from point A to point Z, and when it comes to logical thinking, we seldom take the same route.

Some of us are free-form, intuitive thinkers who reach our conclusions by creative and unpredictable means; others are linear, point-by-point processors who approach their convictions in a more deliberate fashion.

Nowhere do these differences become more apparent than in conflict. You may attempt to lead your partner step-by-step down the unerring path to your inescapable conclusion, only to find that she has ignored the path entirely and is cutting a trail through the woods, arriving (of course) at a conclusion all her own. What did you expect? If only she would think the way *you* think. If only she would be more *logical* . . .

Asking your partner to think like you do is no different than asking her to see colors the way you see them. We have to allow one another the freedom to proceed according to our own style of thinking, and focus on our conclusions rather than our means of getting there.

INSIGHT
Of course, no man is entirely in his right mind at any time.
—*Mark Twain*

CONFIRMATION BIAS: "THAT'S JUST WHAT I THOUGHT YOU'D SAY."

We sometimes treat our partners as if they were a jigsaw puzzle. As we learn more about them over the years, we add pieces to the puzzle until a picture begins to form—a picture of the person as we believe them to be. Just a few more pieces, we tell ourselves, and our picture

SEVEN common red buttons

1
Don't be childish.

2
That's not fair.

3
Let's be logical about this.

4
Be reasonable.

5
You started it.

6
You're just like your mom/dad.

7
You're so sensitive.

INSIGHT
Remember, your reality isn't the only reality.
—*Carol Clifton, Ph.D.*

will be complete.

In conflict, when values, views, and opinions are being shared, it's as if our mate is handing us pieces to add to our puzzle. Some of the new pieces seem to fit our picture and some do not; when they do not, we tend to reject them in favor of those that do. In other words, we all tend to listen for thoughts and ideas that fit our preconceived notions about our mates. This tendency is what communication scholars call "confirmation bias."

The problem with confirmation bias is that it allows no new information into the equation. It fails to consider the complexity of our mates as human beings, and it fails to recognize that all of us are changing over time. We have to listen carefully to our partners and consider all of the information they offer about themselves, regardless of whether it fits our mental picture. We have to be careful not to become more attached to our mental image than to reality itself.

PASSIVE AGGRESSION: "I HAVE NO IDEA WHAT YOU'RE TALKING ABOUT."

"Passive aggressive behavior," writes psychiatrist Ross Campbell, "is an expression of anger that gets back at a person indirectly. Mild examples of this are procrastination, dawdling, stubbornness, intentional inefficiency, and 'forgetfulness.'" Passive aggression is an attempt to punish your mate by dragging your heels or undermining his efforts. Passive aggression is emotional sabotage, and expert practitioners learn to camouflage their attacks so artfully that they appear to be trying to help even while they are seeking to destroy. That's why Ross Campbell calls passive aggression "absolutely the worst way to express anger," the virtual opposite of an open, honest, and direct approach.

He's says he's listening as best he can, but he just can't

> ### INSIGHT
> You don't marry one person; you marry three: the person you think they are, the person they are, and the person they are going to become as the result of being married to you.
> —*Richard Needham*

The Word
A constant dripping on a day of steady rain and a contentious woman are alike; he who would restrain her restrains the wind, and grasps oil with his right hand.

PROVERBS 27:15–16

seem to understand her. She says she's trying to do what he wants, but it's always one step short of what he asked for. He agreed not to do that anymore, but—oops! He forgot. Passive aggression is a real crazy-maker, one that can put the game of conflict on permanent hold. It's hard to work together when one of you is secretly a saboteur.

INDIRECT ARGUMENT: "I WAS JUST KIDDING."

If we push someone, he's likely to push us back. If we merely "bump into" someone, we get the same effect, and there's much less chance of retaliation. We can do the equivalent in conflict. Instead of directly confronting our mates, speaking clearly and directly about our frustrations, we often try to get our point across indirectly through humor or sarcasm. If our mates take the hint, we've made our point. If not, we just keep turning up the volume; a little more biting sarcasm, a little bolder humor. Either way, there's less chance of rejection or reprisal because our mates never consider our words as a true message. If they start to take offense, we were only kidding—weren't we?

> ### The Word
> Just as damaging as a madman shooting a deadly weapon is someone who lies to a friend and then says, "I was only joking."
> PROVERBS 26:18–19 NLT

> ### The Word
> The heart is more deceitful than all else and is desperately sick; who can understand it?
> —JEREMIAH 17:9

The problem with indirect argument is that it asks your mate to do all the work. You drop a hint, and he picks it up—or does he? If he doesn't, you may find yourself growing angry at his thickheadedness, but why? How much attention should he pay to a quick one-liner or a casual aside?

If you have something on your mind, say so clearly and directly. Tell your mate what's bothering you, and tell him what you want him to do differently. If you want your mate to treat your concerns with the respect and attention they deserve, first treat them that way yourself.

Indirect argument conducted in public or in front of friends is even worse. When you haven't honestly confronted your mate in private at home, your relationship has an undercurrent of anger brewing. When

SEVEN kinds of disconfirming messages

1. IMPERVIOUS RESPONSE
Completely ignoring the other person's message

2. INTERRUPTING RESPONSE
Beginning to speak before the other person is finished speaking

3. IRRELEVANT RESPONSE
Making comments totally unrelated to what the other person was just saying

4. TANGENTIAL RESPONSE
Abruptly steering the conversation in a new direction

5. IMPERSONAL RESPONSE
Making distant, intellectual statements instead of interacting on a personal level

6. AMBIGUOUS RESPONSE
Communicating in a vague or indefinite way

7. INCONGRUOUS RESPONSE
Communicating so that your verbal and nonverbal messages deny or contradict one another

—Adapted from Interplay *by Adler, Rosenfeld, Towne, and Proctor, 360–61*

there is an irresistible opening for a jab in front of children or friends, you sometimes take it, laughing as though it was all in fun—but discover later that it wasn't fun for your mate at all.

ATTRIBUTING MOTIVATIONS: "YOU DO THAT JUST TO SPITE ME."

As we said before, communication is a multichannel event—and some of us have more channels available than others do. Those who are skilled at picking up nuances of voice, face, and posture are sometimes tempted to make the ultimate deduction: what's going on in the heart behind the message.

But the simple fact is, no one but God knows what's really going on in the speaker's heart—sometimes, not even the speaker himself knows. No matter how skilled or intuitive you are, your guess is exactly that—a guess. A good guess, perhaps an experienced guess, but a guess nonetheless. If you forget this, your attitude of certainty about your mate's motives may generate a whole new conflict. "Don't tell me what's going on inside my head" is a comment you can look forward to hearing regularly.

You may think you *know* why your mate said or did something; if so, it's best to keep it to yourself for now and talk instead about things you can both observe.

DISCONFIRMING MESSAGES: "I'M NOT LISTENING."

Remember, the chief goals of conflict are better understanding and greater intimacy. To reach those goals, we need to enlist the aid of a series of reassuring messages such as "I hear you," "I understand," "That makes sense," and "I don't blame you for feeling that way."

But sometimes, when we're angry or stubborn or unwilling to reconcile, we use what communication scholars call "disconfirming

------

TIP—INSTEAD OF TELLING YOUR MATE WHAT HIS MOTIVE WAS, ASK HIM FOR HIS MOTIVE. "WHY DID YOU DO THAT?" THEN YOU CAN SAY, "I APPRECIATE YOUR MOTIVE, BUT TO ME IT CAME OUT MORE LIKE . . ."

INSIGHT
Our second year together, when the word divorce slipped into arguments as the ultimate trump card, we agreed to disarm that power. We promised never to wield the word as a threat or a weapon.
—Philip Yancey in Christianity Today

messages." Through words or facial expressions or body language, we communicate to our mate, *I'm not listening, You're boring, I'm tired of this conversation,* or *I just don't care.*

Think of a conversation like a trip across Europe, with checkpoints and border crossings all along the way. At each checkpoint we stop and search for signs of our mate's verbal or nonverbal approval; if we get the go-ahead—*I hear you, I understand, That makes sense*—then we proceed. But all it takes is a disconfirming message or two to cut the trip short.

FIGHTING DIRTY

The final category of Penalties and Fouls is what we simply call "fighting dirty." Fighting dirty will cause you to do far more than miss a turn or go back three spaces; fighting dirty will end the discussion altogether—and sometimes the relationship as well.

Name-calling

Some words are so derogatory, so loaded with rage and contempt, that they can bring a conversation to a screeching halt. You may be sorry you called your mate those names later, and you may sincerely apologize. But even if your partner forgives you, those words may come to mind for years. Forgiving and forgetting are two different things.

Some words deserve to be permanently removed from your personal dictionary—and if you're not sure what they are, just ask your mate.

Escalation

Escalation is the threat of moving the conflict to an even higher level if your partner won't back down. For many, the fear of increased hostility puts an end to the discussion. It also puts an end to understanding and intimacy.

INSIGHT
In destructive conflicts, the participants rely heavily on power to get what they want. "Do it my way, or else" is a threat commonly stated or implied in dysfunctional conflicts. Money, favors, friendliness, sex, and sometimes even physical coercion become tools for forcing the other person to give in. Needless to say, victories won with such power plays don't do much for the relationship.
—From Interplay *by Adler, Rosenfeld, Towne, and Proctor,* 392

INSIGHT
You have not converted a man because you have silenced him.
—John Morley

Using the D word

The word *divorce* is like a trump card, something thrown down at a climactic moment for the shock or fear that it creates. The problem is, used over and over, the word loses its ability to shock; it becomes less of an imaginary threat and more of a real consideration. The word should be eliminated from your vocabulary.

The Word

In the same way, you husbands must give honor to your wives. Treat her with understanding as you live together. She may be weaker than you are, but she is your equal partner in God's gift of new life. If you don't treat her as you should, your prayers will not be heard.

1 PETER 3:7 NLT

Physical threats or violence

The ultimate foul is physical violence. "Violence," writes Isaac Asimov, "is the last refuge of the incompetent." No one is so incompetent at conflict resolution that violence becomes necessary. Brutality is the most shortsighted of solutions: You may get your way, but at the price of intimacy, trust, respect, and even love itself. Violence is never appropriate—not a push, not a shove, not a tight arm squeeze—no violence of any kind, *ever.*

All of these Penalties and Fouls appear at first glance to say, "MOVE AHEAD TWO SPACES." They all seem to be shortcuts, handy techniques that will save you the hassle of wading through a messy disagreement and speed your way to the goal. And they are shortcuts, but they lead to the wrong goal: the goal of victory, avoidance, or revenge. It's important to keep the true goal of the game in mind if you want to avoid setbacks, tangents, or frustrating delays.

! **Just a reminder to turn to the appendix where you can create your own rules for fighting fair based on what you've found helpful in this chapter.**

15

Being Your Own Referee

"Stop saying, 'That's not what you meant!'
I'll tell you what I didn't mean!"

BEING YOUR OWN REFEREE

The referee is easy to spot at any athletic event. He's the one blowing the whistle or throwing the flag or making mysterious hand signals. He's the guy with the striped shirt. He's the one in charge, and everybody knows that you don't mess with the referee, because he's the one who can hand you a yellow card, call a technical foul, or even shout, "You're outta here!" And if he does, you are outta there, because in any competition the referee is the final authority.

TIP—BE PATIENT IN LEARNING TO APPLY YOUR NEW RULES; YOU MAY HAVE SPENT YEARS PRACTICING THE OLD ONES.

The referee always has to be where the action is. He has to stand or run or skate along with everyone else. But at the same time, he has to be careful not to become a part of the action, because he's not really a part of the game. In fact, we could say that a referee has two chief responsibilities: to stay involved and to stay out of the way. When the referee does his job well, he's almost invisible.

Make no mistake; a person has to *learn* to be a good referee. Referees have schools, training camps, and practice sessions just like the athletes do. The same is true in the game of conflict. If we're going to serve as our own referees, we need to learn to do it right. Welcome to training camp! As your own marital referee, you have three chief responsibilities.

KNOW THE RULES

A referee is not a counselor, a lawyer, or a judge. His job is much more focused than that. His duty is to enforce a very specific set of rules, and he needs to know those rules inside out. At a critical moment, no one wants to hear a referee say, "Well, I don't know. I suppose it's all in how you look at it." He needs to *know,* and so do we when it comes to conflict.

But what are the rules we need to enforce? That's the whole point of this book: to give couples a chance to agree together on their own rules of engagement. We're suggesting certain basic principles that we think apply to every couple, and then we're encouraging you to agree together on additional rules of your own.

> **TIP**
> IN THE MIDDLE OF A
> CONFLICT, IF YOU DISAGREE
> ABOUT THE MEANING OR AN
> APPLICATION OF ONE OF YOUR
> RULES, SET THE RULE ASIDE
> AND DISCUSS IT LATER.
> DON'T LET A RULE BECOME A
> TANGENT IN YOUR DISCUSSION.

Two principles will help as you work together on those rules. First, *the time to determine the rules is before a conflict begins*. The middle of a war is no time to try to host the Geneva Convention. If you wait until a conflict is under way to discuss your guiding principles, the principles will just become a part of the disagreement. The time to address the topic of rules and regulations is when you have cool heads, calm spirits, and goodwill. In other words, work out your rules before they matter.

The second principle to remember is that *you both have to agree on the rules*. When we talk about the need for a referee, we're not encouraging one of you to start blowing the whistle every time your mate steps out of bounds. If you do, it will look to your mate like nothing more than an attempt to assert authority or control the conversation, and that will get you nowhere. But how can you both be co-referees? Doesn't somebody have to be the final authority? Yes—the *rules* are the final authority, and that's why it's important that you agree on them together. In a disagreement, it's much better to be able to say, "Remember, we agreed not to . . ." than "I thought I told you not to . . ." or "I thought you said you wouldn't . . ."

STAY INVOLVED

In an athletic event, the athletes are focused on playing the game, but the referee is focused on how the game is being played. That's our job as marital referees: to not only participate in the disagreement but to also pay attention to how the disagreement is taking place.

> **TIP**—DON'T BE SURPRISED IF YOU FEEL SOME ANGER TOWARD YOUR OWN RULES. THAT'S JUST FRUSTRATION; YOUR RULES ARE HELPING YOU FIND A NEW WAY TO COMMUNICATE WITH YOUR MATE, AND THAT'S NOT ALWAYS EASY.

FIVE
good **refereeing
techniques**

1
Refer to your rules
gently and graciously.

2
Call your own fouls
quickly and humbly.

3
Thank your mate
for trying to follow
your rules.

4
Don't let the rules
become the topic
of discussion.

5
Do everything you can
to keep an atmosphere
of goodwill.

Communication scholars call this practice *metacommunication.* "Metacommunication is communication about communication," writes Julia Wood. "For example, John might say, 'I think maybe we're getting sidetracked in this discussion,' or Shannon might say, 'I think we're avoiding talking about the real issue here. . . .' Couples who manage conflict effectively use metacommunication to keep discussion on track, and then they return to the topics at hand" *(Interpersonal Communication,* 301).

In a marital disagreement, we serve as both participants *and* referees. There are two tracks going at once: We talk about the topic, and—when necessary—we talk about the way we're talking. As participants, we might say things like:

"I don't agree with you. I see things very differently."
"That isn't what I meant. Let me explain it another way."
"I really don't like it when you do things like that."

But as referees, our comments will focus on the conversation itself:
"We agreed not to use the word *stupid.*"
"We're beginning to raise our voices."
"We said we would try to stick to one topic at a time."

Notice that each of the referee's comments begins with the same magic word: *We.* That word is critical! Remember, being a good referee is not enforcing rules to control the conversation (You're talking too fast; I don't like that word; Don't raise your voice to me). Being a good referee is simply reminding each other of what you *both* agreed to do (and not do) in advance.

Like all good referees, we need to be where the action is, and in a conflict the action is taking place on several fronts at once: words, attitudes, actions, gestures, and facial expressions. To be good referees we have to pay attention to all of them, because all of them can potentially escalate or derail a conflict. That's why an observant referee will sometimes say:

"It doesn't help when you roll your eyes like that. We said we wouldn't do that."

"That sounded sarcastic. Remember what we agreed about sarcasm?"

"Let's try to stick to one subject like we said."

A good referee has to know the rules and stay involved—but she has a third responsibility that's just as important.

STAY OUT OF THE WAY

As Julia Wood said, the goal of metacommunication is to "keep discussion on track"—to control anger, avoid tangents, and keep moving toward the goal. But the truth is, sometimes metacommunication itself can be a tangent. When we focus *too much* on the way we're talking, the disagreement can shift from the players to the referees. We began by disagreeing about an issue, but now we're disagreeing about the way we're fighting. Some improvement!

In fact, studies show that that's exactly what happens when the referee gets too involved in the game. "Couples who manage conflict ineffectively often become embroiled in metacommunication and can't get back to the issues," writes Julia Wood. "Excessive metacommunication is more likely to block partners than to resolve tensions cooperatively" (Wood, 301).

Keep in mind the role a referee plays in an actual athletic event. As we said before, when the referee does his job well, he's almost invisible. His job is not to interfere with the game, but to do only as much

FIVE *bad* **refereeing techniques**

1
Read your rules with anger or indignation.

2
Make up new rules as you go.

3
Bring up rules only when your mate is in violation.

4
When a rule isn't clear, insist on your own interpretation.

5
Expect your rules to take over when your attitude goes sour.

TIP—DON'T BE SURPRISED IF ONE OF YOUR RULES TURNS OUT TO BE UNHELPFUL OR EVEN COUNTERPRODUCTIVE. NOT EVERYTHING WORKS IN PRACTICE THAT LOOKED GOOD ON THE DRAWING BOARD. JUST AGREE TOGETHER TO REVISE IT OR THROW IT OUT. REMEMBER, THIS IS A PROCESS OF TRIAL AND ERROR.

TIP—TAKE A MINUTE FOR A POSTGAME INTERVIEW. ASK, "WHAT WORKED FOR US, AND WHAT DIDN'T? DO YOU THINK WE SHOULD CHANGE ANY OF OUR RULES OR ADD ANY NEW ONES?"

as is necessary to allow the game to continue. When you sense that too many references to the rules are beginning to generate anger or resentment, just back off and return to your role as player.

The best way to ensure that your refereeing doesn't become a part of the argument is to focus on refereeing *yourself*. Even when you say, "*We* agreed . . ." it can still sound to your partner like a veiled correction or an attempt to control the conversation. But your partner will never complain when you want to point out your own violations. A good referee should be quick to call a foul on himself. He might say things like:

"I shouldn't have said that. I meant to say . . ."

"Wait, what I said was too harsh."

"I'm sorry, that was too sarcastic."

But what happens when your partner refuses to play by the rules? What do you do when you find yourself blowing the whistle so often that your disagreement sounds like a marching band? That's when a referee needs to . . .

KNOW WHEN TO POSTPONE THE GAME

We do not believe that every disagreement can be brought to a peaceful and productive conclusion. Due to harsh start-ups, distracting tangents, and plain old orneriness, sometimes a conflict is doomed to generate more heat than light.

But neither do we believe that conflicts should be avoided. As we said before, unresolved conflicts are like toxic waste that can accumulate and create an environment that is poisonous to the growth of oneness, intimacy, and love. When a conflict begins to go astray, the goal is not to bury it, but to postpone it for a fresh start at another time.

As referees we want to keep an eye out for those communication spirals, situations

INSIGHT

Whether on the road or in an argument, when you see red it's time to stop.

—*Jan McKeithen*

when the general atmosphere of the conversation is—to use a fitting metaphor—going down the drain. There are six common indicators of a downward spiral:

- Increasing anger
- **Increasing defensiveness**
- Increasing attacks on character rather than actions
- **Increasing sarcasm or contempt**
- Increasing confusion over the original issue
- **Increasing momentum**

TIP—TRY CALLING A HALFTIME IN YOUR DISCUSSION. TAKE A SHORT BREAK TO COOL DOWN AND GET SOME DISTANCE FROM THE PROBLEM.

When you sense these six indicators coming together, it's time to postpone the discussion. If you insist on pushing ahead, you may end up saying things you regret—things that will become the topics of other conflicts in the future.

Remember, when a referee postpones the game, he's also responsible for getting it started again. When you agree to postpone, make it your last order of business to also agree on when you'll try again.

Is there a time to cancel the game altogether? Are there situations where it's impossible to be your own referee?

KNOW WHEN TO SEEK AN OUTSIDE REFEREE

There are five specific situations when it may be wise to seek the assistance of an outside referee: a friend, a mentor, a pastor, or a professional counselor.

1 *When there is violence or uncontrollable anger.* We should think of conflict the way we think of fire: a powerful tool that can cause great harm if misused. The fundamental rule for handling fire is "Safety first." Conflict is no different. First and foremost, a conflict has to be safe. If you feel frightened or endangered by your mate, then it's definitely time to seek outside help. Do it right away.

2 *When there has been past trauma or abuse.* Sometimes a dis agreement taps into hurts or fears from our distant past. When that's the case, you may find yourselves unable to untangle the current conflict. *Why is this such a big deal to her? Why does he blow up like that?* If you come from an abusive or traumatic past, a counselor can help you to deal with your pain at its source.

3 *When your mate is unwilling to make or keep rules.* If your mate is unwilling to even discuss guidelines for conflict, or if he disregards them completely once a conflict is under way, then forget the rules for now. There's an underlying source of anger or resentment here, and an outside advisor may be able to help you understand it.

4 *When the relationship itself is in a downward spiral.* When a relationship reaches a toxic level of anger, bitterness, and resentment, no simple set of rules will put it back on track. When the downward spiral begins to look like a tornado, it's time to address the issues *behind* the issues, and an outside referee can help.

5 *When you're deadlocked on a recurring issue.* Sometimes, despite our best efforts, we just can't find a way around a specific disagreement. We may have blind spots. In those cases, it helps to enlist the aid of someone with a fresh perspective, someone with a level of objectivity that the two of you lack.

A final tip for aspiring referees: Keep the rules in front of you. A football referee is not ashamed to reach into his hip pocket and pull out an actual rule book; neither should we be. That's why, at the end of this book, we've included a place for you to create your own rule book. This is the place for you to record the words you don't want to say, the gestures you don't want to use, and the attitudes you don't want to display. We encourage you to copy those pages and keep them handy. Conflict is a time when passions rise and memories fall; why try to remember what you agreed upon all those months ago? Keep your personal rule book nearby and refer to it when necessary—but only when necessary. Remember, the rules are your reminder, not your master.

16

Preventing Conflicts Before They BEGIN

"The National League Playoffs have been interrupted by this important announcement..."

DOWNS

PREVENTING CONFLICTS BEFORE THEY BEGIN

The buzzword in health care these days is preventive medicine—*taking conscious steps to avoid an illness or adverse condition altogether. It only makes sense; miracle drugs are wonderful, but the only miracle they really perform is to return you to normal. Some miracle! Why not skip the cure and just remain healthy and happy?*

The same question applies to conflict. All that we've said so far about fighting fair is a cure for a malady that's already in progress. Wouldn't it be better to skip the cure and just stay happy? Is there such a thing as preventive medicine when it comes to disagreement? Is there a way to prevent a conflict before it begins?

Scott Stanley and his associates, in their book *A Lasting Promise,* describe a preventive maintenance program that can do wonders for any marriage:

> We believe relationships have two kinds of commitment: dedication and constraint.
>
> A commitment characterized by personal dedication refers to the desire of an individual to maintain or improve the quality of the relationship for the joint benefit of both partners.... In contrast, a commitment characterized by constraint refers to forces that keep individuals in relationships whether or not they're dedicated. (Stanley et al., 164)

Stanley claims that there are two kinds of glue that help to hold a marriage together: *dedication* and *constraint*. Constraint is the term for the *external* forces that help keep marriages intact: legal codes, social norms, family expectations, and societal pressures. Don't underestimate the value of constraint. As Judith Viorst once wrote, "One advantage of marriage is that, when you fall out of love with him or he

falls out of love with you, it keeps you together until you fall in again."
There is great sustaining power in the legal commitment and the covenant before God we all made at the altar.

But Stanley wants us to understand the even greater power of dedication. Dedication comprises all the *internal* desires to make a marriage succeed, "not only to continue in the relationship but also to improve it, to sacrifice for it, to invest in it, to link personal goals to it, and to seek the partner's welfare, not simply one's own" (Stanley, 164).

> ### INSIGHT
>
> **Chains do not hold a marriage together. It is threads, hundreds of tiny threads, which sew people together through the years.**
>
> —*Simone Signoret*

Dedication and constraint work together to make a marriage last, but dedication is what makes it fulfilling. Doesn't your heart just leap for joy when you recall that your spouse cannot leave because he is legally bound to stay? In the movie *Jerry Maguire,* Jerry is in a relationship with a single mom named Dorothy. The relationship is beginning to get serious, and Jerry wants Dorothy to know that he won't be just another love-'em-and-leave-'em suitor.

"I'm not a guy who runs," he assures her. "I *stick.*"

Her reply: "I don't need you to 'stick.'" *Don't talk to me about constraints,* she was saying. *Speak to me of your dedication.*

"What do you want?" he asks. "My soul?"

"Why not?" she replies. "I deserve that."

We *all* deserve that. It's dedication—the knowledge that your partner loves you, desires you, and wants your marriage to succeed that keeps those home fires burning. But don't forget: Unlike constraint, dedication requires constant renewal. Without it, "today's dedication becomes tomorrow's constraint" (Stanley, 174).

What does all this have to do with preventing conflict? In chapter 2 we said that when we invest in everything and everyone but *us,* marriage eventually becomes a cold, lonely, and disappointing business— and that's when the storm clouds of conflict begin to gather. But when you and your mate take time to be together, when you renew your *dedication* to each other, there is a confidence in the relationship that

---

FIVE forms of dedication that help keep a marriage growing

1. DESIRING THE LONG-TERM
An expectation and a desire for the relationship to last

2. THE PRIORITY OF RELATIONSHIP
The importance given to the relationship relative to everything else

3. WE-NESS
Viewing the relationship as a team rather than two separate individuals who each focus on what's best for themselves

4. SATISFACTION WITH SACRIFICE
A sense of satisfaction in doing things that are for the partner's benefit

5. ALTERNATIVE MONITORING
Choosing not to dwell on tempting alternatives to the marriage

—*Adapted from* A Lasting Promise *by Scott Stanley et al.,* 169–73

FIVE
essential factors for a good relationship

1. COMMUNICATION
As you are willing and able to discuss the issues (as opposed to fight, debate, defensively argue, or lob grenades), you have a chance for resolution.

2. SENSE OF HUMOR
Are you able to laugh at your own sensitivities, pomposities, and mountainous molehills? Is your ego involved too much in what you do?

3. COMMITMENT
Are you really, truly committed to this relationship, or are you just there?

4. FLEXIBILITY
Can you listen to the other side? Can you bend, compromise, give in sometimes?

5. LOVE AND RESPECT
Do you care for and about each other and show it daily?

—Adapted from Leo Buscaglia, quoted in How to Keep People from Pushing Your Buttons *by Albert Ellis and Arthur Lange, 124–26*

forms a buffer against misunderstanding and miscommunication. It's a buffer made of positive attitudes that we described before:

- **I'm confident of your love for me, even if you haven't told me lately.**

- I know you're trying, even when it doesn't show.

- **I know you mean well, even when it comes out wrong.**

- I think the best of you, even when you fail.

- **I trust you, even when I'm not there with you.**

We said that when you firmly believe—when you really *feel*—that your mate loves, values, and respects you, it's easier to overlook the minor oversights and annoyances that happen every day. To put it another way: By developing dedication, couples can prevent conflicts before they ever begin.

What does it mean to "develop dedication" on a daily basis? Here are five practical suggestions to help you break out of that business partnership and get a marriage going again.

SHOW UP FOR THE MARRIAGE

To succeed at any event, you have to show up for the game. You showed up for the wedding; why miss the rest of the marriage? The first and foremost principle of dedication-building is that *you have to find time to be together*.

Before you glibly check this item off your To-Do list, allow us to clarify: Developing dedication requires a certain *kind* of time together. It requires getting your mind and your body in the same room at the same time. It means choosing activities other than watching DVDs. Do something that will cause you to actually (gasp) *interact* with each other. It means time to slow down and time to focus on anything other than the job, the kids, or next week's carpool schedule. It means time to be together

INSIGHT
Kindness has converted more sinners than zeal, eloquence, or learning.
—*Frederick W. Faber*

as lovers and not just as business partners.

This kind of time is hard to find. If it's been a while since the two of you have shown up for the marriage, you may find at first that it's even harder to know what to do with the time when you find it!

TALK ABOUT SOMETHING ELSE

For years we made the mistake of taking our calendars with us when we went out to lunch. We would end up spending every minute of our time discussing the details of next week's schedule: the kids, the dentist, the car repair, the dry cleaning . . .

When was the last time you asked your mate what she thought about art (and not taking the kids to the art museum)? About politics (and not changing your voter registration)? About God (and not next week's church activities)? When was the last time you talked to your mate about anything other than business?

> *TIP*—SET ASIDE TEN MINUTES A DAY TO CATCH UP WITH YOUR SPOUSE. ASK, "WHAT WAS THE BEST THING ABOUT YOUR DAY? WHAT WAS THE MOST CHALLENGING?"

Life is busy, and it takes a lot of planning and coordination just to get things done. But to become more dedicated to your mate, you need to know more *about* your mate. From time to time, you need to talk about something else.

HEAP ON ENCOURAGEMENT AND PRAISE

Samuel Johnson once said, "Praise, like gold and diamonds, owes its value only to its scarcity." We've discovered a fundamental principle of marital economics: Conflict increases as praise and encouragement decline.

Women often report that in the absence of praise, they tend to assume their husbands' disapproval. *If I were doing it right, you would have said so; something must be wrong.* But men often take the opposite

----

TIP—MAKE A DATE WITH YOUR MATE AT LEAST EVERY TWO WEEKS. DO SOMETHING FUN WHERE YOU CAN TALK AS WELL.

THIRTEEN decisions that help a couple become intimate companions

1. I will lock the escape hatch and throw away the key.

2. I will be intentional.

3. I will make our relationship a priority.

4. I will revisit my expectations.

5. I will champion you.

6. I will nurture my private life.

7. I will be responsible and reliable.

8. I will be honest.

9. I will connect with you.

10. I will reveal myself to you.

11. I will allow you to influence me.

12. I will work through issues with you.

13. I will forgive.

—Adapted from Lifemates *by David and Janet Congo, table of contents*

approach. For them, the absence of criticism implies approval. *If you were doing it wrong, I would have told you; everything's OK.* He offers the silence of approval, but she hears the silence of complaint. A husband who is perfectly pleased with his wife, but hasn't bothered to *say* so, may find an unexpected conflict waiting in the wings.

"Marriage should be a duet," Joe Murray writes. "When one sings, the other claps." Invest in dedication by heaping on praise and encouragement. If you don't praise and encourage your wife, who will? It's a thankless and critical world out there, and this is a golden opportunity you have in your partner's life.

MAKE A LIFESTYLE OF GRATITUDE

The poet Goethe once wrote, "No married couple can calculate the debt they owe each other. It is an infinite sum and can only be paid in eternity." Gratitude is simply the verbal expression of that immeasurable debt.

The Bible highly recommends the giving of thanks—not merely the *feeling* of thankfulness but the audible communication of that gratitude to another. The expression of gratitude not only encourages the receiver; it has a powerful perspective-correcting effect on the sender too. It drowns out grumbling and complaining, and it shifts the person's focus; it makes the half-empty glass suddenly appear half-full.

The Word
So then let us pursue the things which make for peace and the building up of one another.
—ROMANS 14:19

The man who says "I can't complain" just lacks imagination. You can always find something to gripe about, but we all have plenty to be thankful for too, especially when it comes to our mate. It's all a matter of perspective. When you remember to say "Thank you" to your mate, you're also saying "I notice, I care, and I need you." Those are potent messages, and they're powerful antidotes against feelings of discouragement and disapproval.

LET GRACE ABOUND

Proverbs 19:11 says, "People with good sense restrain their anger; they earn esteem by overlooking wrongs" (NLT). "Overlooking wrongs" is what *grace* is all about.

One of the most common sources of conflict in marriage is conflict itself; we grow angry and cross because we're fighting all the time. When every minor annoyance or irritation becomes the topic of a discussion, a downward spiral begins. Why is she so *picky*? Why does he have to complain about *everything*?

As the proverb suggests, it makes good sense to restrain our anger and simply let some things go. When we do that, we "earn esteem" from our partners; they begin to think of us as generous and forgiving, and that makes it easier for them to be generous and forgiving in return.

But how can you overlook something that really bothers you? You can't—and you shouldn't—if it's a serious offense. We're recommending that you work to create an atmosphere in your home where *little* things don't bother you as much. Don't underestimate the power of this principle; life is *filled* with little things.

In a sense, grace is not a separate principle at all, but the culmination of our previous four. When we spend time together as friends and lovers, when we heap on encouragement and praise, and when we make a habit of saying "Thank you" even for little things, the atmosphere of generosity and goodwill that results is *grace*.

Every couple needs to learn how to fight fair. But remember, one of the most common sources of conflict in marriage is conflict itself. You may have even experienced a little friction with your mate

---

INSIGHT

Although we often have little choice of what happens to us, we surely have some choice as to what happens in us.

—*Evelyn Underhill*

INSIGHT

Research has shown that one of the greatest threats to a marriage occurs when spouses regularly interpret each other's behaviors negatively.... Begin to give your spouse the benefit of the doubt until you've had a chance to talk with him or her about whatever is troubling you. You may find yourself overly upset for nothing.

—*From* How to Act Right When Your Spouse Acts Wrong *by Leslie Vernick, 41*

INSIGHT

Happiness does not depend on outward things, but on the way we see them.

—*Leo Tolstoy*

EIGHT rules to drastically improve a relationship

1

Show genuine enthusiasm when you greet the person.

2

Show respect.

3

Be supportive.

4

Give her the benefit of the doubt.

5

Let her know you appreciate her.

6

Give her the chance to contribute to your life.

7

Talk about what is bothering you.

8

Share yourself and open up a bit with this person.

—Adapted from Make Peace with Anyone *by David Lieberman, 162–64*

discussing our book! Why do we have to talk about this? Why is this a problem for us? Why is it so hard?

Conflict begets conflict, and that's why every couple's focus should be on preventing conflict before it ever begins. Talk to each other, encourage and thank each other, and let grace abound, and you'll find you're creating an atmosphere where conflict doesn't grow.

! **Just a reminder to turn to the appendix where you can create your own rules for fighting fair based on what you've found helpful in this chapter.**

17

The Game That Never ENDS

"We can't afford to remodel the house right now,
so I'm planning to redo Bob instead."

THE GAME THAT NEVER ENDS

If you're newly married, you may have felt a little discouraged reading this book. We keep using words like conflict, argument, and heated disagreement. But so far, all the heat in your relationship has been the good kind. To you our book sounds overly pessimistic, like an omen of bad things to come. Right now you may feel like the soldiers in Raiders of the Lost Ark *who made the mistake of peeking into the sacred ark. Already you can feel the good times beginning to melt away. . . .*

INSIGHT

Love at first sight is easy to understand. It's when two people have been looking at each other for years that it becomes a miracle.

—*Sam Levenson*

Relax. Because this book focuses exclusively on conflict, we know that we may have painted a depressing picture of marriage. That's the last thing we want to do—and that's why we've chosen to end our book with four points that will help put everything back in proper perspective.

EVERYONE IS INCOMPATIBLE

Now isn't that encouraging?

"In every marriage more than a week old, there are grounds for divorce," Robert Anderson writes. "The trick is to find, and continue to find, grounds for marriage." If you haven't yet discovered it, you and your mate have profound differences of opinion on life, liberty, and the pursuit of happiness—and you'll discover even more differences as you grow older together.

Here's the best-kept secret in marriage today: "Compatibility" is not a lack of differences; it's the attitude *toward* your differences. In one sense, everyone is incompatible

INSIGHT

Another flaw in the human character is that everybody wants to build and nobody wants to do maintenance.

—*Kurt Vonnegut*

because everyone is different; but in practice, you're not incompatible unless you allow your dissimilarities to produce anger, bitterness, and resentment.

IT ONLY GETS BETTER FROM HERE—IF YOU WORK AT IT

Despite almost everything our culture will tell you, the best romance is found *inside* marriage, and it can get better over time. Our culture treats romance as a kind of chemical reaction that's most explosive when the chemicals are fresh. On the contrary, romance is like a *nuclear* reaction that can be sustained indefinitely—but not without continual refueling. "Almost no one is foolish enough to imagine that he automatically deserves great success in any field of activity," writes Sydney Harris. "Yet almost everyone believes that he automatically deserves success in marriage." No one *deserves* success in marriage—but with God's help success is available to anyone who is willing to work for it, and making the commitment to resolve conflict peaceably is a critical part of that work.

CONFLICT INCREASES WHEN LIFE GETS SERIOUS

Some studies claim that our enjoyment of marriage changes over time according to a predictable pattern. We begin marriage with a very high level of satisfaction, but in a few years that contentment begins to dip. Our satisfaction with marriage continues to decline until it finally bottoms out, and it remains in this gutter of discontent for several years before suddenly beginning to rise again.

How do we account for this multiyear trough of frustration and dissatisfaction? Think of the changes and demands that come with the first several years of marriage: little things like bearing children, making budgets, changing careers, dealing with in-laws, moving across the country, raising teenagers, and experiencing your own midlife crisis—if you can find the time. These are the years when life gets serious. The number and significance of the decisions you have to make together increases geometrically, and it happens while you yourselves are struggling with your own dwindling energy. Your responsibilities reach their peak just as your resources bottom out, and it's in this exhausted and stressed-out condition that you have to make *decisions*.

It's no wonder that conflict increases during the middle years of marriage and why it subsides in the years that follow. As friends of

INSIGHT
Story writers say that love is concerned only with young people, and the excitement and glamour of romance end at the altar. How blind they are. The best romance is inside marriage; the finest love stories come after the wedding, not before.
—*Irving Stone*

INSIGHT
More marriages might survive if the partners realized that sometimes the better comes after the worse.
—*Doug Larson*

ours once told us, "We have a lot less to fight about now that the kids are gone."

You don't have to wait for the kids to leave to improve your marital satisfaction—but you may have to change your approach to conflict. When life gets serious, disagreements will increase, and that's when your skills as good referees will be most important.

USE THE RULES; DON'T LET THE RULES USE YOU

Advertising pioneer David Ogilvy once wrote, "Rules are for the obedience of fools and the guidance of wise men." That's an important reminder at the end of a book on rule-making. Some of us like rules because written regulations are a substitute for having to think. Once the rules are in place, that's all there is to it—just follow the letter of the law.

But in marriage it's the *spirit* of the law that makes all the difference. Allow us to reiterate one last time the principle we have emphasized throughout this book: *Success in conflict requires more than a set of rules.* It depends even more on attitudes like humility, generosity, gentleness, and a genuine desire to work things out. The ultimate rule is the Golden Rule; no list of dos and don'ts can ever replace it, and no amount of self-effort will fulfill it apart from the power of God.

Then what good is the list of rules you have drafted together as you read this book? The key is in that little word—*together*. Your list of rules and personal fouls is not a judge and jury demanding your obedience; it's a set of goals you've agreed upon *together* to serve as guidelines when conflict begins and the skies grow dark and cloudy. Keep your rules handy and refer to them when necessary, but don't let the rules become a part of the conflict. Use the rules—but don't let the rules use you.

CONFLICT IS THE GAME THAT NEVER ENDS

Nobel Peace Prize winner Elihu Root once wrote, "Men do not fail; they stop trying." When it comes to achieving peace in marriage, the only real failure is to no longer make the attempt. The greatest barrier we face in learning to fight fair is our own discouragement over past attempts.

In Philippians 3:13, the apostle Paul writes about his own experience with past disappointment and failure: "No, dear friends, I am still not all I should be, but I am focusing all my energies on this one thing: Forgetting the past and looking forward to what lies ahead, I strain to reach the end of the race and receive the prize for which God, through Christ Jesus, is calling us up to heaven" (NLT). Chuck Swindoll writes about this passage:

> I know human nature well enough to realize that some people excuse their bitterness over past hurts by thinking, "It's too late to change. I've been injured and the wrong done against me is too great for me ever to forget it. Maybe Paul could press on—not me!" A person with this mind-set is convinced that he or she is the exception to the truths of this chapter and is determined not to change because "life has dealt him or her a bad hand."
>
> But when God holds out hope, when God make promises, when God says, "It can be done," there are *no exceptions*. With each new dawn there is delivered to your door a fresh, new package called "today." God has designed us in such a way that we can handle only one package at a time . . . and all the grace we need will be supplied by Him as we live out that day. (*Improving Your Serve*, 77)

*Conflict is the game that never ends—but there is hope as long as you do not stop trying. Remember, **conflict is essentially a spiritual activity**, and God is a God of peace and grace. With His help, you can learn to "fight fair" and to love your mate even in the midst of your differences.*

INSIGHT

The art of living lies less in eliminating our troubles than in growing with them.

—*Bernard M. Baruch*

INSIGHT

Most couples contend with some trait or circumstance that won't seem to go away, no matter what they do. Courage calls us to accept the malady, as Paul did his mysterious affliction, and lean hard on God's grace for the strength to endure what we neither deserve nor entirely welcome.

—*Diane Eble in* Marriage Partnership *Magazine*

INSIGHT

Character consists of what you do on the third and fourth tries.

—*James Michener*

APPENDIX A: OUR RULES

SETUP *(Chapter 6)*

Places to talk that just don't work for us:_____

_____

_____

_____

_____

Times to talk that just don't work for us: _____

_____

_____

_____

_____

Our best *places* to talk:

At home: _____

_____

_____

_____

Away from home: _____

_____

_____

_____

Our best *times* to talk:

At home: _____

_____

_____

_____

Away from home: _____

_____

_____

_____

OUT WITH THE OLD RULES *(Chapter 8)*

What old, bad conflict habits do we agree to break?

(Example: We agree not to walk out in the middle of an argument.)

_____

_____

_____

_____

_____

_____

_____

_____

_____

_____

_____

_____

_____

_____

_____

_____

_____

_____

_____

_____

_____

_____

_____

_____

_____

_____

PASSING THE DICE *(Chapter 9)*

What do we agree to do to improve the way we listen to each other?

We will stop: _____

_____

_____

_____

_____

We will begin to: _____

_____

_____

_____

_____

What do we agree to do to improve the way we speak to each other?

We will stop: _____

_____

_____

_____

_____

We will begin to: _____

_____

_____

_____

_____

What do we agree to do to make sure we both take turns? _____

_____

_____

_____

_____

_____

MASTERING THE ENDGAME *(Chapter 10)*

What pseudoapologies do we agree to stop using? _____

_____

_____

_____

_____

_____

What do we agree to do to improve the way we apologize to each other?

We will stop: _____

_____

_____

_____

_____

We will begin to: _____

_____

_____

_____

_____

What do we agree to do to become more forgiving toward each other?

We will stop: _____

_____

_____

_____

_____

We will begin to: _____

_____

_____

_____

_____

_____

FOLLOW-THROUGH *(Chapter 11)*

What do we agree to change so that some of our disagreements will no longer occur?

_____

_____

_____

_____

_____

_____

_____

_____

_____

_____

_____

_____

_____

_____

_____

_____

_____

_____

_____

_____

_____

_____

_____

_____

WHO LET THE DOGS OUT? *(Chapter 12)*

What do we agree to do to express anger more productively? _____

_____

_____

_____

_____

_____

_____

_____

_____

_____

We will stop expressing anger in these ways:_____

_____

_____

_____

_____

_____

_____

_____

_____

_____

_____

Instead, we will try to: _____

_____

_____

_____

_____

_____

_____

_____

_____

_____

_____

PUTTING IT ALL TOGETHER *(Chapter 13)*

What do we agree to do differently in our general approach to conflict?

_____

_____

_____

_____

_____

_____

_____

_____

_____

_____

_____

_____

_____

_____

_____

_____

_____

_____

_____

_____

_____

_____

_____

_____

_____

_____

_____

_____

PENALTIES AND FOULS *(Chapter 14)*

These are the words, attitudes, and actions that we agree are our personal fouls:

Blame: "This is all your fault."

We agree not to: _____

_____

_____

_____

_____

The question of origins: "You started this."

We agree not to: _____

_____

_____

_____

_____

History lessons: "This is like the time when you . . ."

We agree not to: _____

_____

_____

_____

_____

Reading from the record: "Your exact words were . . ."

We agree not to: _____

_____

_____

_____

_____

_____

Defensiveness: "It wasn't my fault."

We agree not to: _____

_____

_____

_____

Reversal: "Me? What about when you . . . ?"

We agree not to: _____

_____

_____

_____

Comparison: "Why can't you be like Mike?"

We agree not to: _____

_____

_____

_____

Button-pushing: "Why do you have to act so childishly?"

We especially agree not to use these words or phrases:_____

_____

_____

_____

Analogies: "This problem is like an oak tree."

We agree not to: _____

_____

_____

_____

Logic: "Why can't you be more rational?"

We agree not to: _____

_____

_____

_____

Confirmation bias: "That's just what I thought you'd say."

We agree not to: _____

_____

_____

_____

Passive aggression: "I have no idea what you're talking about."

We agree not to: _____

_____

_____

_____

Indirect argument: "I was just kidding."

We agree not to: _____

_____

_____

_____

Attributing motivations: "You do that just to spite me."

We agree not to: _____

_____

_____

_____

Disconfirming messages: "I'm not listening."

We agree not to: _____

_____

_____

_____

Fighting Dirty

Name-calling: We especially agree not to use these words or phrases:

_____

_____

_____

_____

Escalation: We agree not to:_____

_____

_____

_____

Using the *D* word: We agree not to: _____

_____

_____

_____

Physical threats or violence: We agree *never* to: _____

_____

_____

_____

PREVENTING CONFLICTS BEFORE THEY BEGIN *(Chapter 16)*

What do we agree to do together to improve the general atmosphere in our marriage?

_____

_____

_____

_____

_____

_____

_____

_____

_____

_____

_____

_____

_____

_____

_____

_____

_____

"Yes, I am the vine; you are the branches. Those who remain in me, and I in them, will produce much fruit. For apart from me you can do nothing." (Jesus in John 15:5 NLT)

APPENDIX B: ATTITUDE IS EVERYTHING

In chapter 5 we said, "Many contests are won or lost before they even begin; it all has to do with the mind-set you bring to the game." If you want to improve your attitude going into a conflict, take a few minutes to reflect on these challenging and encouraging passages of Scripture.

- "This is my command: Love one another the way I loved you. This is the very best way to love. Put your life on the line for your friends." (John 15:12–13 THE MESSAGE)

- Is there any encouragement from belonging to Christ? Any comfort from his love? Any fellowship together in the Spirit? Are your hearts tender and sympathetic? Then make me truly happy by agreeing wholeheartedly with each other, loving one another, and working together with one heart and purpose. (Philippians 2:1–2 NLT)

- Don't be selfish; don't live to make a good impression on others. Be humble, thinking of others as better than yourself. Don't think only about your own affairs, but be interested in others, too, and what they are doing. (Philippians 2:3–4 NLT)

- You must make allowance for each other's faults and forgive the person who offends you. Remember, the Lord forgave you, so you must forgive others. (Colossians 3:13 NLT)

- Love is patient and kind. Love is not jealous or boastful or proud or rude. Love does not demand its own way. Love is not irritable, and it keeps no record of when it has been wronged. It is never glad about injustice but rejoices whenever the truth wins out. Love never gives up, never loses faith, is always hopeful, and endures through every circumstance. (1 Corinthians 13:4–7 NLT)

- Don't use foul or abusive language. Let everything you say be good and helpful, so that your words will be an encouragement to those who hear them. (Ephesians 4:29 NLT)

- Don't repay evil for evil. Don't retaliate when people say unkind things about you. Instead, pay them back with a blessing. That is what God wants you to do, and he will bless you for it. (1 Peter 3:9 NLT)

- Get rid of all bitterness, rage, anger, harsh words, and slander, as well as all types of malicious behavior. Instead, be kind to each other, tenderhearted, forgiving one another, just as God through Christ has forgiven you. (Ephesians 4:31–32 NLT)

The next time a difficult discussion is about to begin, sit down together, hold hands if you can, and pray this simple prayer together. If your mate is unwilling, pray it alone. Remember, "Don't worry about anything; instead, pray about everything. Tell God what you need, and thank him for all he has done" (Philippians 4:6 NLT).

Lord, we know that You have graciously forgiven us for the things that we have done wrong. Help us to remember that and to generously share that forgiveness with each other. Help us to understand each other; give us kind, gentle, and gracious words; help us to remember Your presence here and to speak and act accordingly. Give us humility, control our anger, and leave us with a greater love for each other when our conversation is done.

SOURCES CITED

Ronald Adler, Lawrence Rosenfeld, Neil Towne, and Russell Proctor, *Interplay: The Process of Interpersonal Communication* (Harcourt Brace, 1998).

David Augsburger, *Caring Enough to Confront* (Regal, 1981).

Tom Barrett, *Walking the Tight Rope: Balancing Family Life & Professional Life* (Business/Life Management, 1994).

Ross Campbell, *How to Really Love Your Teenager* (Victor, 1993).

Tim and Julie Clinton, "How 'Disaffection' Starts," *Moody Magazine*, Nov/Dec 2002, 25.

Nancy Cobb and Connie Grigsby, *How to Get Your Husband to Talk to You* (Multnomah, 2001).

David and Janet Congo, *Lifemates: A Lover's Guide for a Lifetime Relationship* (ChariotVictor, 2002).

John Cook, ed., *The Book of Positive Quotations* (Fairview Press, 1997).

Linda Dillow, *Calm My Anxious Heart* (NavPress, 1998).

James Dobson, *Emotions: Can You Trust Them?* (Regal, 1980).

Tim and Joy Downs, *One of Us Must Be Crazy . . . and I'm Pretty Sure It's You* (Moody, 2010).

Albert Ellis and Arthur Lange, *How to Keep People from Pushing Your Buttons* (Citadel Press, 2003).

Sybil Evans and Sherry Suib Cohen, *Hot Buttons: How to Resolve Conflict and Cool Everyone Down* (Cliff Street Books, 2000).

Timothy W. Galwey, *The Inner Game of Tennis* (New York: Random House, 1997).

John M. Gottman and Nan Silver, *The Seven Principles for Making Marriage Work* (Three Rivers Press, 1999).

Alice Gray, Steve Stephens, and John Van Diest, *Lists to Live By: The Second Collection* (Multnomah, 2001).

Alice Gray, Steve Stephens, and John Van Diest, *Lists to Live By: The Fourth Collection* (Multnomah, 2002).

Art Hunt, *A Weekend with the One You Love* (Multnomah, 1997).

David Lieberman, *Make Peace with Anyone* (St. Martin's Press, 2002).

Fred Lowery, *Covenant Marriage: Staying Together for Life* (Howard Publishing, 2002).

Chuck Lynch, *I Should Forgive, But . . .* (Word, 1998).

Wayne Martindale and Jerry Root, ed., *The Quotable Lewis* (Tyndale, 1989).

Stormie Omartian, *Lord, I Want to Be Whole* (Nelson, 2000).

Dennis and Barbara Rainey, *Two Hearts Praying as One* (Multnomah, 2002).

Reader's Digest Association, *Reader's Digest Quotable Quotes* (Reader's Digest, 1997).

Mark Rosen, *Thank You for Being Such a Pain: Spiritual Guidance for Dealing with Difficult People* (Crown Publishing, 1999).

Ken Sande, *The Peacemaker: A Biblical Guide to Resolving Personal Conflict* (Baker, 1997).

Scott Stanley, Daniel Trathen, Savanna McCain, and Milt Bryan, *A Lasting Promise: A Christian Guide to Fighting for Your Marriage* (Jossey Bass, 1998).

Douglas Stone, Bruce Patton, and Sheila Heen, *Difficult Conversations: How to Discuss What Matters Most* (Penguin, 1999).

Charles R. Swindoll, *Improving Your Serve* (Word, 1990).

Richard and Rita Tate, *11 Reasons Families Succeed* (Hensley Publishing, 2002).

Leslie Vernick, *How to Act Right When Your Spouse Acts Wrong* (Waterbrook, 2001).

Joanna Weaver, *Having a Mary Heart in a Martha World: Finding Intimacy with God in the Busyness of Life* (Waterbrook, 2000).

Ed Wheat, *Love Life* (Pyranee, 1980).

Julia Wood, *Interpersonal Communication: Everyday Encounters* (Wadsworth, 1999).

H. Norman Wright, *Communication: Key to Your Marriage* (Regal, 2000).

RECOMMENDED RESOURCES

WEBSITES

FamilyLife: http://familylife.com

Dr. Gary Chapman: www.garychapman.org/; www.5lovelanguages.com

Drs. Les and Leslie Parrott: www.realrelationships.com/

Gary Smalley: http://gosmalley.com/

BOOKS

For information on Tim Downs novels, please visit http://timdowns.net.

Dan Allender and Tremper Longman, *Bold Love* (NavPress).

Dr. Dan B. Allender and Tremper Longman, *Intimate Allies* (Tyndale).

Dr. Gary Chapman, *The Five Love Languages: The Secret to Love That Lasts* (Northfield).

Gary Chapman and Jennifer Thomas, *The Five Love Languages of Apology: How to Experience Healing in All Your Relationships* (Northfield).

Tim and Joy Downs, *Fight Fair!: Winning at Conflict Without Losing at Love* (Moody).

Emerson Eggerichs, *Love & Respect: the Love She Most Desires; the Respect He Desperately Needs* (Integrity).

Shaunti Feldhaun, *For Women Only: What You Need to Know about the Inner Lives of Men* (Multnomah).

Shaunti Feldhaun, *For Men Only: A Straightforward Guide to the Inner Lives of Women* (Multnomah).

Nancy Sebastian Meyer, *Talk Easy, Listen Hard: Real Communication for Two Really Different People* (Moody).

Drs. Les and Leslie Parrott, *The Complete Guide to Marriage Mentoring* (Zondervan).

Drs. Les and Leslie Parrott, *Trading Places: The Best Move You'll Ever Make in Marriage* (Zondervan).

Dennis and Barbara Rainey, *Staying Close: Stopping the Natural Drift toward Isolation in Marriage* (Thomas Nelson).

Ken Sande and Tom Raabe, *Peacemaking for Families: A Biblical Guide to Managing Conflict in Your Home* (Tyndale).

Mitch Temple, *The Marriage Turnaround* (Moody).

Gary Thomas, *Sacred Influence: How God Uses Wives to Shape the Souls of Their Husbands* (Zondervan).

Gary Thomas, *Sacred Marriage: What if God Designed Marriage to Make Us Holy More than to Make Us Happy?* (Zondervan).

Dr. H. Norman Wright, *Communication: Key to Your Marriage* (Regal).

ACKNOWLEDGMENTS

Thanks to our dear friends and family who encouraged us during the process of writing this book: Tom and Linda Barrett, Mark and Julie Bontrager, Ben and Janet Burns, Bill and Laura Burns, Dan and Julie Brenton, Bobby and Ann Clampett, Doug and Patty Daily, Mark and Erin Donalson, Steve and Myra Ellis, Doug and Teri Haigh, Bill and Rese Hood, Jim and Renee Keller, Kent and Kim Kramer, Jon and Noonie Fugler, Tim and Noreen Muehlhoff, Glenn and Beth Melhorn, Al and Diane Meyer, Mike and Renee Seay, Dave and Sande Sunde, Sam and Carol Thomsen, J. T. and Enid Walker, and John and Susan Yates. We appreciate all of your prayers on our behalf.

And thanks to our editor, Cheryl Dunlop, for her insights and contributions to the text, and to Pam Pugh for 2010 revisions.

ONE OF US MUST BE CRAZY...
AND *I'M PRETTY SURE IT'S YOU*

In this companion to *Fight Fair!*, Tim and Joy Downs capture the heart of marital differences. Rather than another "men and women are different" book, this fun and fresh approach explores why certain types of arguments recur. You may think you're fighting about a vacation or whether Junior needs a bicycle helmet—but the actual, underlying issues are about Security, Loyalty, Responsibility, Caring, Order, Openness, and Connection.

Discover what's really going on and why you're thinking, *One of us must be crazy...* and what to do about it!

MOODY
PUBLISHERS

www.MoodyPublishers.com